Brett Arends writes for the *Daily Mail* in London. He has also written for *Private Eye*, the *Daily Telegraph*, *The Economist* and the *Express*. He was educated at Gonville & Caius College, Cambridge, where he took a double first in History, and Christ Church, Oxford. He worked as a management consultant with McKinsey & Co before escaping to journalism. He lives in Pimlico, central London.

Spread Betting:

A Football Fan's Guide

Brett Arends

A *Time Warner* Paperback

First published in Great Britain in 2002
by Time Warner Paperbacks

A CIP catalogue record for this book
is available from the British Library.

ISBN 0 7515 3411 0

Typeset in Times by Palimpsest Book Production Limited,
Polmont, Stirlingshire
Printed and bound in Great Britain by
Clays Ltd, St Ives plc

Time Warner Paperbacks
An imprint of
Time Warner Books UK
Brettenham House
Lancaster Place
London WC2E 7EN

www.TimeWarnerBooks.co.uk

Contents

Acknowledgements

Where do I start? To the 'experts' on Wall Street and in the City of London, my deepest thanks. You did not know it, but without you this book would never have been written. Your folly first showed me just how wrong markets can be.

I am grateful to Alan Samson, Catherine Hill and Philip Parr at Time Warner Books, who did a superb job in revising and correcting the manuscript in about the time it takes for Real Madrid to score a goal. It is a cliché in every book's Acknowledgements to say that the remaining errors are mine – but it is not until you write one of your own that you realise just how true that is.

My thanks to Paul Austin, Wally Pyrah, Jonathan Sparke, David Garbacz and the lads at the spread betting firms for their assistance, and to Paul Evangelou, James Mitchell and the Country Pub regulars for making it such a civilised place to watch the game.

Finally, I want to thank all my friends, whose support has been more important to me over the years than I can adequately express. For their role while this book was being prepared I want to thank in particular Caroline Bates, Andrew Roberts, Geoffrey Levy, and of course my brother Andrew.

For my mother

1

In the Tunnel

Everybody has an opinion. Rio Ferdinand is the new Bobby Moore. Ferdinand is overrated. Man U are in trouble. You can never write them off. Emile Heskey is vital to England's attack. Heskey is a waste of space. Real Madrid are the best club side ever assembled. Juventus are going to win the Champions League. Juan Sebastian Veron is the biggest waste of money since the Dome.

The best argument for spread betting is that people can put their money where their mouth is – indeed, if it were compulsory, we might all be spared a fair amount of hot air. You can bet for or against any team, or almost any player, in any competition. Goals, Goal Times, Bookings, Corners, Season Points – the list of markets offered by the spread firms is bewildering. They can offer more than a hundred different bets on a single game.

It also allows you a little financial participation in football without doing anything as foolish as buying shares in your club. Owen was reported to have been paid £1.56 million by Liverpool in the 2001/2 season, when the scampering superstar scored 28 goals. So each goal cost Liverpool's owners £56,000. You can buy them for a fiver. If that's not value, I don't know what is.

It can become compulsive. I've found myself racing home in a taxi after work trying to make sense – very quickly – of team sheets and recent form data, prices pages from the bookmaker's, and this morning's copy of the *Racing Post*. Once, as I tried to calculate Bayer Leverkusen's corner average by the dim light overhead, my mobile phone rang. It was a City friend who was away in Ireland visiting clients. 'I'm standing in Dublin airport right now,' he said, desperately. 'My plane takes off in fifteen minutes. I've just got a chance to place a bet. What do you fancy for the match?'

I became interested in spread betting when the stock market turned dull. I write for the City pages of the *Daily Mail*. In the late 1990s the market was the best game in town. Technology and telecom shares skyrocketed to absurd levels. It was free money. Characters I had known at school, and to whom I would not have lent the price of a cup of tea, saw their ventures 'valued' at hundreds of millions of pounds (one of them managed to sell out at the peak, collecting £20 million). And then, right at the end, came the easiest money of all. In the final frenzy anything that wasn't a dotcom was virtually being given away for free. Wise people moved in and scooped them up with both arms.

In the aftermath I turned my attention to spread betting. I have never been able to get my head around fixed odds, with its 7–4s and Yankees and tired old men hanging out in the local betting shop smoking rolled cigarettes. But spread betting uses a simple pricing system which operates much like any other market. You buy things – the number of goals in a match, the number of points Newcastle are likely to get over the course of the season – in the hope they will go up. If they do, you win. If they fall, you lose. Easy.

The bookies make a prediction – for example, that Newcastle will end the season with 60 points. Let's say you think the Magpies will get more. If you buy at £100 a point and they get 5 points more, finishing with 65, you make £500 and you can take a holiday in the south of France. Of course, if they only get 55, you lose £500 and you will have to settle for somewhere less glamorous. Newcastle, say. I love this simplicity, but there are other advantages to the spreads. One is that you can turn this trade on its head. Instead of buying something hoping it will go up, you can sell it, hoping it will go down. If you sell Newcastle's season points at 60 at £100 a point, and they only get 55, you can make your £500 that way. You can make money by successfully predicting someone will have a rotten season. Does it get any better than that?

Selling, or 'going short', is counter-intuitive. We understand the idea of buying something for £5 hoping to sell it later for £10. The idea of selling it for £10 first, hoping you can fill the order later by buying it for only £5, takes some getting used to. But it is one of the great tricks of spread betting.

Another advantage is that you don't need to back winners. You can make money if a team simply does better than expected. It can come eighth: if everyone else thought it would come twelfth, and you bought expecting it to do better, you're in profit.

You can trade in spread bets 'in the running' – during the game, the season or the tournament. Prices are constantly updated, so if events move in your direction, you can close out at a profit long before the final whistle. If you bought before the rise, now you can sell the bet back and take your money. You can even close your bet before the game kicks off, selling it back if you have second thoughts or the circumstances change. Usually you will have to pay the spread, though sometimes money pouring in from other gamblers will move the prices enough to let you get out at no cost, or even at a small profit. Collecting your profit on a game before the kick-off has a particular charm.

These are, for me, the strongest attractions of spread betting. The weakest claim for it is that 'the more right you are, the more money you make', as one of its inventors sometimes puts it. That uncertainty, and the possibility of almost unlimited risk, is what usually puts people off. It does not help that some of the easiest spread bets to explain, such as total goals in football (or total runs in cricket), can offer this sort of open-ended commitment. But there are plenty of ways to avoid it, for example by betting on a market called the 'Win Index' in football instead of goal Supremacy. I happen to dislike the idea of unlimited risk and do my best to avoid it; it's not difficult.

The bookies now set hundreds of prices, covering every televised game and different leagues and tournaments around the world. This keeps them busy. And prices have to be constantly updated to reflect events. During a game, the price on the likely number of goals it will see is whittled down with each passing goalless minute, and raised again whenever anyone scores. Markets on season points have to be updated after every game.

In practice the bookies do not offer one price, but two. In the above example, if they think Newcastle will get 60 points, they will let you buy at 61, and sell at 59. The difference, the 'spread', gives them their cut on the two-way traffic. Some of these spreads can be ridiculously large. This is most true on some of the most popular markets, such as the likely number of goals in a match ('Total Goals'),

and a team's expected winning margin ('Supremacy').
Markets with fat spreads are, of course, best avoided.

As I became more involved, so I became more curious
to know whether the market for football was as irrational,
and as easy to profit from, as shares can be. The short
answer is that it's not, at least not quite. But it does follow
similar patterns. Once you know which forces are setting
the prices, you know how rational they are. Then you
know where to look for value.

Some years ago a professional punter revealed on TV
that he had made good money every year simply by selling
bookings before each match. After the programme aired
other amateur punters piled in and did the same thing to
try to emulate his success. But the bookmakers simply
lowered the prices. The magical free money did not mate-
rialise. Or rather, it did – for the bookies.

In the stock market there are all sorts of measures, such
as price-to-earnings ratios and net asset value, which give
you some idea of whether a share is cheap or expensive
in relation to its fundamentals. To bet intelligently on football I needed some similar basic grounding in facts. This
is the only way to know whether a bookmaker's price is
high or low. After many months' digging around on the
internet, and with some help from a few friendly moles
within the spread betting firms, I found some answers.

This book explains the markets and the betting process
in detail, using examples from real matches. I use smaller
bets as examples simply because they are easier to follow.
The principles are the same whether you are betting £1 a
point or £1,000. I have usually described winning bets.
Be warned: if you gamble, there will be times when that
will seem far from normal. There have been periods when
I forget what a winning bet looked like.

The Appendices are for reference, covering aspects of

football spread betting and including various charts and tables.

Beating the market on football can be a tougher game than beating the City. Prices are still largely set by professional market-makers. They do their research and they know their football. Happily, this is starting to change. As the spread firms grow, so they are slowly becoming more conservative, letting the weight of money influence prices and taking their cut on the two-way trade. It is early days, but this is set to continue. The more you are betting against other, amateur punters, the easier it is for the shrewd speculator to gain an edge.

Nevertheless, football punters are better at seeing value than most City fund managers. This is largely because they are betting their own money. Fund managers are betting yours. They are driven by fashion. They will chase yesterday's news and then wonder why they underperform the stock market average year after year. This is like running back and forth between bus stops, chasing the last bus to leave. You'll never get home.

Companies – such as the collapsed energy company Enron – are able to hide profits and losses behind a variety of ruses. Football is more transparent. Goals, bookings, wins and losses are there for everyone to see. There are no 'proforma' goals. No one claims in May to have had a winning season 'before exceptional items'. No football team has ever tried to pass off goals scored as the same as goal difference. Bad managers are bundled out quickly, instead of hanging on to do more damage.

The stock market is respectable. Gambling isn't. This is a curious paradox. If you invest in stocks in a balanced and conservative fashion, picking sound companies, diversifying and making long-term choices, it should not prove a gamble. But this is not what many people do. Instead they speculate, taking risks on penny shares, punting on unproven businesses and what they hope will be the market's next big move. This is gambling, pure and simple. People do it for the same reasons – the fun and the hoped-for profit, in that order. In America gambling is heavily restricted. In most parts of the country casinos, corner betting shops and slot machines are illegal. Even telephone and on-line betting are banned. This may have spurred the dotcom bubble, as for many Nasdaq was the only casino in town.

Obviously spread betting on sports is no substitute for investing. But it is preferable to simple speculation. Reaching an informed view about the Aston Villa defence is rather easier than reaching one about, say, an obscure biotech company. It also has another enormous advantage: it's much more fun.

2

Win, Lose or Draw

Let's make a deal. I'll give you £25 if your team wins today. I'll give you £10 if they draw. You'll get nothing if they lose. How much would you pay me up front to take the bet?

The amount you should risk depends, of course, on who is playing, and where. If you were backing Roma in the Stadio Olimpico in Serie A over the 2001/2 season, if you paid £21 a time you would have come out ahead. Most of the time you would have got your £25 back. They drew just four times, and did not lose once. If you were betting on Real Madrid at the Bernabeu, you could also have paid up to £21, and Bayern Munich at home, £20. Arsenal's away record exactly matched Real's at home, winning fourteen games, drawing five and losing none. But although it was worth £21 a game on the road, it was worth no more than £17 at home, where they dropped three games. The difference between the top and bottom clubs is as stark as you would expect. Leicester away from home were worth no more than £7 a time, and in Italy Venezia just £6.

Variously called 'the Win Index', 'the 25' and 'the Pony',

this is one of the simplest and most popular markets offered by the spread firms. They will give 25 points if your team wins, 10 if it draws, and nil if it loses. If you bet at £10 a point, your potential cash return is £250, £100, or, obviously, zero. Buying Manchester United at 16 at £10 a point is to bet £160.

The Win Index is easy to compare to fixed odds betting, which can be helpful for those making the transition (Table 2 in the Appendices compares the prices to fixed odds). It also offers strictly limited risk, so there are no nasty surprises. You know in advance how much you can lose. If you buy Crystal Palace at 6 at £10 a point, you can lose only £60. They can lose 17–0 and have three men sent off and you still lose only £60. It is an automatic each-way bet. You can bet against a team with one easy trade. And, most importantly, like most spread bets, you can trade it actively during the game.

Manchester United are away at Aston Villa in a third-round FA Cup tie. The Red Devils have bounced back from a dismal string of losses in late autumn and are in dangerous form, winning six games in a row. With their Premiership title hopes alive again, they are dreaming of another treble. Meanwhile, Villa have just one win in their past ten games, and five losses. Manchester have outscored Villa this season by a margin of 60 per cent. Their top four (Van Nistelrooy, Solskjaer, Beckham and Giggs) have scored more goals between them than Villa's top twelve, their top two more than Villa's top four. Yet the visitors are priced at just 16.5 to buy in the Win Index (and 15 to sell). Pro-favourite opinion may have been dampened by Leeds's recent surprise loss to Cardiff. The price looks cheap. Convinced Man U will beat an indifferent Villa team, I buy at £10 a point.

The match does not go exactly according to plan. Before

the start comes the news that key United players, Ruud Van Nistelrooy, Ryan Giggs and Fabien Barthez, the keeper, are all on the bench with injuries. This is half a Manchester United team. That is the risk of betting well in advance of kick-off, and is the reason why it is usually better to open your account at the last minute.

The first half ends with no score. Soon after the break, Villa's Ian Taylor capitalises on a quick ball through to give the home side the lead. One goal is neither here nor there, but two minutes later there is a disastrous mix-up at the back and Man U defender Phil Neville heads the ball into his own goal. It is now 2–0 to the home team. My bet looks lost, a painful £165. I can sell my bet back, but the price is now just 1.5 to sell so I would get just £15. It isn't worth it. The bookies, as always during matches, are responding automatically. They might also be trying to make money off panicking punters, desperate to sell out at whatever cost.

Others, who had bided their time, go the other way. I know of one Man U fan who bought the team at 3 at a thumping £100 a point. And why not? Man U are specialists at famous comebacks. Earlier in the season they went 3–0 down to Spurs in the first half before storming back after the break to win 5–3. You can hate them, and many do, but only a fool writes them off easily.

Meanwhile, those who had bought Villa before the game, at just 8.5, can now take their profits. The home side has been marked up to 20.5 to sell. If you bought at 8.5 at £10 a point, you can now sell at 20.5 also at £10 a point. This closes your bet with a juicy £120 gain. Nothing that happens after that affects you either way. This is just like buying a share and then selling it. You don't really care if the company goes bust the following day. You're out. But if you are going to do this tonight, do it quickly. Along the sidelines at Villa Park an allegedly injured Ruud Van Nistelrooy is getting ready to come on as a substitute for Manchester.

Van Nistelrooy's arrival galvanises the team. Man U, who had been in disarray moments before, are suddenly on the front foot and pressing forward. Villa, fatally, show signs of looking to hang on for the victory. For fifteen minutes their strategy looks like paying off. But then, in the 77th minute, Solskjaer makes the breakthrough for the visitors, conjuring a chance out of nowhere and finishing beautifully with a shot through the knees of Villa's keeper, Peter Schmeichel. Suddenly the visitors are back in business. The home crowd stop cheering. The prices start whipsawing, and I consider closing out my United bet for a smaller loss, but decide to hold on. A few minutes later, Van Nistelrooy chests a cross into the penalty box, turns and thumps the ball into the back of the net to level the game. Man U are still making all the running. A couple of minutes later they break again. The ball is passed through to Van Nistelrooy on the right wing who boldly dashes around a charging Schmeichel and slots the ball away. The score is now 3–2, with eight minutes of regular time left.

My bet is now heavily back in profit. The game seesaws. Villa are fighting back. They are down the Man U end of the pitch and may yet equalise. If Manchester hang on for the win their price in the Win Index will settle at 25 points. But a Villa equaliser would knock that to 10 points, costing me heavily. I close out my bet at 22.5, collecting £60 profit. I am giving up another £25 potential profit but this is a sensible move. In the event there is no further score and Manchester United collect yet another famous comeback victory.

*   *   *

Home-field advantage matters. By just how much is surprising. Across all leagues here and in Europe, home teams are almost twice as likely to win as the visitors. The hosts win roughly half of all matches, the away team about one-quarter, and one-quarter are draws.

The figures vary by league, but not by much. In England home teams over the past five seasons have won 47 per cent of games, away teams 27 per cent. Draws are also more common than many think, accounting for another 27 per cent. In the major continental leagues the home-field advantage is even stronger. Home teams in La Liga and the Bundesliga have won 49 per cent of the time in recent seasons, those in Serie A 48 per cent. In Italy, where the atmosphere in the stadia can be particularly powerful, visitors have won just 23 per cent of games.

Partly this is psychological: the home team is boosted by the crowd, and is used to their surroundings and the pitch. They have not spent the previous night in a hotel room or travelling. Home advantage is also, doubtless, self-reinforcing. A weak team playing at home is more likely to believe in its chances, even against a much stronger opponent. A weak team playing away might assume even before kick-off that it is doomed. On the other hand, a strong team away might be content to take a draw, even against a team at the bottom of the table.

This creates opportunities for some profitable trades. Weak teams are often worth backing at home, especially if they are facing a heavily favoured opponent and are offered on the cheap. There is a better chance of a draw than many expect. Put simply, you can often make money buying Manchester United (or Real Madrid) at home, and selling them on the road. The prices frequently will not vary as much as they should.

In the Win Index, Premiership teams playing at home

are worth a price of 14.3 on average and the away team just 9.3. The figures in the top continental leagues reflect the bigger home-field advantage. A look at the past five seasons in the Premiership shows that teams finishing in the top five merit, on average, a Win Index price of 18 when playing at home. If you bought them consistently below that price over the course of a season, you would make money. However, when playing away the risks of a draw, and even the occasional shock loss, rise sharply. You would have to buy them consistently below 14 to make money. The 2001/2 season was remarkable in more ways than one. The top teams fared much worse than usual at home, Arsenal dropping three and Man U six, but better on the road. As a result, the top five were worth more on average on the road (17.3) than at home (16.8). This is rare.

As the top clubs do so well over the season, we tend to forget, or downplay, all the minor stumbles. A typical top-five performance might be Liverpool in the 2000/1 season. They finished third with 69 points. Nevertheless, they drew away at Southampton, West Ham, relegation-bound Manchester City, Sunderland and Ipswich, lost on the road to Leeds, Chelsea, Spurs, Middlesbrough, and even at home drew against Sunderland, Middlesbrough and Derby and lost to Ipswich and Leeds. Even in the most successful season of recent memory, Manchester United's 91-point run during 1999/2000, the team dropped the occasional surprise – such as drawing against Everton, Southampton and Sunderland, losing 3–0 to Spurs at White Hart Lane and 5–0 to Chelsea at Stamford Bridge.

Equally, there is a price for the long-term underdogs and it is not zero. Teams ending the season in the bottom five of the table, those plagued by apparent disaster and woe throughout the year, still merit a Win Index price of around 10 when playing at home. Even the weakest teams in recent memory, Leicester in 2001/2 and Nottingham Forest in 1998/9, were worth buying at 7.6 on average when playing in their own stadia. Away, the average for the bottom five slumps to 6.3. In the season when they were relegated, 1999/2000, Wimbledon still managed home wins against Leeds, Sunderland and Newcastle, home draws against Spurs, Southampton, West Ham and Aston Villa, draws away against Newcastle, Villa, Middlesbrough and Arsenal, and – remarkably – draws both home and away against the eventual champions from Old Trafford.

In the second round of the Champions League poorly rated Nantes are at home to heavily favoured Man U. Nantes, with zero points from two games and showing poor form in the French league, are certain to exit the competition. The *Racing Post* marvels that Nantes have even made it into the second round. Manchester are second favourites overall to win the cup. Everyone seems to have written off the French team completely. However, Nantes are playing at home. Furthermore, by now they have nothing to lose. On the morning before the game, the manager says the team are simply going to go out and have fun. Man U, on the other hand, are carrying burdensome expectations. You would consider there is a decent chance of a draw, or even – more remotely – an upset victory for the French team.

In the Win Index, Nantes are priced at 8.5 to buy. This is unattractive. The upside in case of a draw is just 1.5 points. The downside if Nantes lose is 8.5. If you stake £10 a point, you are risking £85 in the hope of making £15 profit from a draw.

However, Manchester United are simultaneously priced at 15.5 to sell (and 17 to buy). The bookmakers offer a Win Index on both teams in a game. Here is value. Instead of buying the underdogs, you can sell the favourites. The concept of selling – going short – can be intimidating to newcomers to spread betting. It needn't be. Selling works in exactly the same way as buying, but in reverse. Instead of betting that the final number will be higher than predicted, you are betting that it will be lower. If you sell at 15.5 and United lose, you make 15.5 points profit. If they draw you make 5.5. If they win, they settle at 25 and you lose 9.5.

The match proves remarkable. Nantes, buoyed by a cheering crowd who had simply come for a good night out, and freed from all expectations, go ahead within ten minutes. The visitors pepper their opponents' penalty box in vain for more than eighty minutes. At this point, if you sold Man U at 15.5 you are looking at a wonderful £155 profit. They look destined to make up at zero, and you will pocket the difference. Towards the end you could cover yourself by buying your bet back at 2, making 13.5 points profit or £135. In injury time, the visitors' pressure finally pays off and they win a penalty, which Ruud Van Nistelrooy converts to level the game. It ends 1–1 and both teams make up at ten. By selling the favourites at 15.5, you collected 5.5 points profit (or £55 at £10 a point). If you had bought Nantes, for the same result you would have made just £15.

Buying one team in the Win Index is not the same as selling the other. If one team wins it collects 25 points, but if the match is drawn the two sides share just 20 points, 10 apiece. When comparing the two, always chose the one which gives you the best result if the match is drawn. This will raise your profits – or reduce your losses – over time. You could also have sold *both* teams. The sell price for Nantes was 7. Add that to Man U's sell price and they come to 22.5. A draw produces 20 points, a win for either side 25. So this gives evens on a draw.

Southampton are at home to Leeds on a Saturday, and the visitors' chances of an emphatic victory look absurdly undervalued by the bookies. Instead of the Win Index, you look at the most popular market in spread betting, that of Goal Supremacy. The bookmakers today are offering Leeds's 'Supremacy' – their likely winning margin, or goal difference – at just 0.3 to sell, 0.6 to buy.

Fractions of a goal throw some people, but these are merely a fiction thought up by the bookies to make it easier to produce a market. Imagine if the Supremacy market were offered purely in terms of whole goals. Leeds would be 0 to sell, 1 to buy, and no one would deal. Leeds would have to win by two goals for buyers to make any money. Similarly, those who took a chance on Southampton by selling Leeds at 0 would need the home team to win. A draw, making up at 0, would merely leave you level. A 1–0 victory to Southampton would produce a Leeds 'Supremacy' of -1. If you had sold at zero at £100 a goal, you would make £100.

A price of 0.3 to 0.6 means the bookies think Leeds are, roughly, just as likely to come away with a draw as they are to win by a single goal. Statistically, the price might be right. If you look at the two teams' recent averages, you would expect Southampton to score 1.05 goals at home to Leeds, and Leeds to score 1.55 goals in reply. But this ignores two key issues. The first, and most obvious, is that the superb Robbie Fowler has just joined the Leeds attack from Liverpool and last match found his feet with the new club by scoring a hat-trick against Bolton. The second is that the recent results are unequal. Leeds's recent figures reflect matches against strong opponents including Newcastle and Chelsea. Southampton beat

Sunderland and Leicester. Southampton are struggling near the bottom of the Premiership, while Leeds are in strong contention near the top.

You buy Leeds's Supremacy at 0.6 at £100 a goal. Leeds play well below their best, while the Saints fail to score from good chances in both halves. However, in the 89th minute Lee Bowyer scores from a through ball from Mark Viduka, and Leeds win 1–0. You bought at 0.6, so your profit is the difference, or 0.4 of a goal. At £100 a goal, this produces £40 profit.

In the Supremacy market home advantage is worth on average 0.43 of a goal. Over ten seasons Premiership teams have scored just over 1.5 goals a game at home and 1.1 goals away. In practical terms this means that in ten games you would expect the home sides to score a total of about 15 goals, the visitors 11. Again, this varies somewhat on the continent but not by much. In Germany the hosts outscore their visitors by 0.55 goals a game. Over 100 games you would expect the home sides' goal difference to be 55. In Italy's Serie A and Spain's La Liga it is 0.5. In the Appendices Table 2 shows the home-field advantage for the major teams in England and on the Continent.

Most Premiership teams finish the season with a positive goal difference at home. Only the bottom four or five teams are likely to end up in negative territory, the team finishing dead bottom typically at nearly -0.8 goals a game. The situation on the road is almost exactly reversed. Typically only the top four clubs will have a positive goal difference away from home. The worst team will finish with an average of around -1.2.

Chelsea play West Ham at Upton Park in an FA Cup fourth-round replay. Honours are even at 1–1 at half-time. In the second half Chelsea dominate possession and create a host of chances but fail to convert. The Hammers go on the counter-attack, and Jermain Defoe heads home a second to make it 2–1. Chelsea bring on two substitutes, Zola and Forssell, adding a striker and raising the stakes. West Ham currently enjoy a one goal lead but their Supremacy price is less, 0.6 to 0.9, so the market gives some chance of an equaliser. You think that will happen, so you sell West Ham's Supremacy at 0.6 at £100 a goal. Ten minutes later Forssell scores, prodding the ball past the keeper in a penalty-box melée. The score is now now 2–2. West Ham's Supremacy price drops to 0 to buy (and -0.3 to sell). So the bookmakers now believe Chelsea have a slightly greater chance of scoring a third time than do West Ham. You can now close your bet for a quick £60 profit by buying Supremacy back at 0. There are good arguments for this. You reason the Blues might take the draw and bring the replay back to Stamford Bridge, while West Ham – fearing exactly that – might go all out for a winner. In the event John Terry rockets home Chelsea's third in injury-time to win the game. If you held on you made £160.

In-the-running trade contains a trap for beginners. You do not trade in and out of a bet at the price on the score-board but at the price in the market at the spread firms, which will reflect what people think the scoreboard will show at the end of the match. If you sold Total Goals at 2 and there are 3 in the first twenty minutes, you can't buy back your bet at 3. By that stage the market price for Total Goals will probably be 5. You would have to deal at that price.

This can be unsettling. During the Ashes cricket series I went short of Mark Ramprakash Runs in the Oval Test at 42. By the time he had reached 40 it was clear he was settling in and hitting well. On paper I had no loss yet: he was still on 40 runs. But if I wanted to close the bet I had to buy it back in the mid-60s. That is what people thought he would make for the whole innings. I was reluctant to take a loss on a bet that was still, on paper, in profit, so I hung on – and quickly regretted it. By the time Ramprakash was in the 60s, his price was in the 80s. I then bought back for a heftier loss.

When people want to bet on the outcome of a match, they tend to prefer the Supremacy market to the Win Index. This is good news for the bookmakers, but bad news for the punters. The bookies' spread between the buy and sell prices is a thumping 0.3 of a goal in the Supremacy market. That is 24 per cent of the average make-up, which is 1.28 goals in the Premiership, 1.24 across all English leagues. You have to cover the spread before you even start making profits, even if you correctly assess which team will have the upper hand. The size of the margin is most apparent when the bookies offer Supremacy at '0.9 to 1.2'. Think about that. If the game ends with a one-goal margin, and 38 per cent of them do, the bookmaker makes money from both the buyers and the sellers. By contrast the margin in the Win Index is just 1.5 points. That is 13 per cent of the average make-up, which, taking into account wins and draws, is 11.8 per team.

Buying Supremacy is so tempting to many because they dream of the big score. It rarely happens. We remember the few that do for obvious reasons, and forget the dull draws and bleak one-goal victories. Two-thirds of Premiership games end with a margin of one or zero. A thumping 86 per cent end with a margin of two goals or fewer. If the buy price for Supremacy is offered above 1, it is best to leave it alone. On the other hand, if the sell price is also offered above 1 it might be tempting to go short.

The Win Index is also a much better market to use for

in-the-running betting. Its far slimmer margins allow you to trade in and out without paying for two extortionate spreads, one when you buy and one when you sell. It also offers limited risk. When a team is battling from behind they are in danger of a counter-attack. If you buy their Supremacy, you risk a double whammy if they fail to equalise and then let in another. With the Win Index, if you buy at 2.5, that's all you can lose. When betting in the running you have to make quick decisions. The game runs on while you call up the bookmaker, and the situation is invariably volatile. Using the Win Index market to bet on the outcome of the match gives you some measure of control. In-the-running betting is doubly dangerous because it is so compulsive.

Real Madrid are playing Deportivo in the final of the Spanish Cup, the Copa del Rey. Everything points to a blowout for the Madrid team. The match takes place in their home stadium, the Bernabeu, where their record is sensational. So far this season, in all competitions, they have won 18 here and drawn only 5. They have not lost at home in over a year. They have outscored their opponents by 62 goals to 15, an average difference of 2 goals a game. Deportivo, by contrast, have a losing away record and have been outscored on the road. They came here two months ago and were soundly thumped 3–1. Today, cup final day, is the exact 100th anniversary of Real's founding. Every bigwig in the country seems to be here for the match. The cameras occasionally cut to them in the pre-match build-up, sitting in the expensive seats looking smooth and chain-smoking.

The prices on Real seem dirt cheap, possibly because most British punters are focused instead on a big domestic match instead. You can buy the home team in the Win Index at 17.5, and sell Deportivo at 6. But I decide to wait and watch ten minutes of the game before taking the plunge.

The match begins slowly, the commentators' brains equally so (sample remark: 'Real Madrid don't hope to win this competition, they don't expect to win this competition, they *demand* to win this competition!'). But it is Deportivo who push forward first, taking the lead after five minutes with a nifty little flick by striker Sergio Gonzalez through the legs of Real's keeper.

Real's price slumps. You can now buy them at just 11 in the Win Index. Prices during the match are updated on a strict formula, based on the current score and the time left to run in the game. A strong home team that goes behind early is a classic in the running buy. Real at 11, one goal down at home with nearly the whole match to play, looks compelling and I buy at £10 a point. A draw, making up at 10, will entail a loss of £10. A defeat will cost £110. A win, making up at 25, will return profits of £140. Many others take the same view and the price on Real ticks up half a point in moments.

Real start making the running in attack. Deportivo are defending superbly, but the dancing feet of Zidane, Roberto Carlos and Raúl threaten constantly. Figo, on the other hand, is clearly not match fit. He has been on the bench for some weeks, is half a yard short of his opponents, and lunges to catch up. In this he resembles the recent form of the Arsenal defender Martin Keown – an ominous sign.

Half an hour passes. Real have two-thirds of the possession, but nothing to show for it. A goal will surely come. The only worry is that they are defending precariously, and are in danger of being caught on the break. I am pondering this danger in the 38th minute when Deportivo stream forward again and Diego Tristan makes it 2–0.

This is trouble. Time and again I would take Real

Madrid to win at home at better than evens when they are just one goal down and there are eighty minutes to play. The commentators remind us they haven't lost at home for fifteen months. But a two-goal deficit, with just under an hour left, is more worrisome.

The price on Real collapses to just 3.5–5. What should you do? Unhelpfully, perhaps, there are two schools of thought. The first suggests you should cut your losses. Buying Real at 11 at £10 risked £110. If you now sell at 3.5, also at £10, you get £35 back, cutting your loss to £75.

There is a better point of view. Forget the £110, which is already committed. Instead, ask yourself a question: if you did not already have a bet on the outcome, would you now buy Real Madrid at 3.5? That is the price at which you can close the bet. Leaving a bet open when you can close it is the same as opening a bet. In the City, where professionals have plenty of experience of losing bets (although usually with your pension money, rather than their own), they call this 'marking to market'.

Madrid are at home, 2–0 down, with nearly an hour to play. If I bought at 3.5 at £10 a point, I would be risking £35. If Real score two I would get back £100, a juicy £65 profit. If they score three and win, I would get back £250. The odds are against them, but this is Real Madrid. I think this is compelling and I keep my bet open.

After the break Real bring on the Argentinian Santiago Solari, an attacking midfielder. This allows Raúl to move forward. They step up the pressure on Deportivo, but the visitors' line holds and time ticks away without a goal. As the home team grows ever more anxious they start leaving space at the back. Deportivo launch a counter-attack, but miss a sitter – a moment of brief, but high, emotion in my flat – which would have made it an unbeatable 3–0 with just over half an hour left. Real are looking less and less convincing, and I start to think seriously about closing my position. The price has fallen to 2.5–4. That looks very low, but with just over half an hour left would I buy at that 2.5? Maybe. It's marginal. That means you should probably avoid making the bet, and if I wouldn't buy it I should not keep it open. But suddenly, in the 59th minute, Madrid's persistence is rewarded as Raúl scores a scrappy goal to make it 2–1. There is half an hour to go.

The price on Real Madrid jumps to 6.5–8. This is one advantage of betting in the running on a favoured team. Punters will grab eagerly at any signs of a comeback and the price will jump higher than it should. This is a cue to get out, selling at 6.5. But I do not have to move immediately. As the Bernabeu comes alive, I can wait a few minutes to see if Real develop momentum. Excitable punters pile into Real, keeping the price high. Yet the home side are making more errors, while Deportivo defend stoutly. The line is holding. Nothing is getting through. Fifteen minutes pass without further excitement, but the price is still 6–7.5. Now is the time to exit. I sell back at 6, taking a £50 loss.

Real fans do not give up easily. In the 90th minute the fourth official signals four minutes of overtime. After three minutes and thirty seconds, with Real still 2–1 down and showing no signs of making the final breakthrough, you can still buy the visitors in the Win Index at 24.5.

Final-second comebacks do occur, but very rarely: 4 per cent of goals occur in what statisticians call the '90th minute', which includes stoppages.* That equates to roughly

---

* In preparing this book I went through the entertaining process of collecting data on all goal times over four Premiership seasons and putting them into a spreadsheet. It is not a process I would wish to repeat. The results, grouped into five-minute intervals, appear in the Appendix, Table 12. And to think you're getting this book for six quid! Cheap at twice the price.

1 per cent per minute of injury-time. But in this case there were just thirty seconds left. Just 0.5 per cent of goals come that often. With 2.6 goals per game on average, that means that over the run of a season you would expect a goal in the final thirty seconds or so just 1.3 per cent of the time, or once every 75 games. It is true that stoppage-time can be dragged out for an extra minute or sometimes two. But Real appeared to have given up and Deportivo were defending like troopers. Assuming a pricing error, I called Sporting Index to check and they confirmed. While we were speaking, Deportivo had a throw-in near the halfway line and the final whistle was blown before I hung up. What was the chance Zidane could snatch the ball from Deportivo, run fifty yards through a network of defenders and score in that time? Hope springs eternal. More remarkable is that it still springs thirty seconds from the end of a tight game.

The final third of a game frequently offers great betting chances. If a team is down by a goal and there are twenty minutes of regular time left, you can usually buy them in the Win Index at around 3.5. With ten minutes to go, this will drop to 2 or even 1.5. Over time this apparently makes sense and profits for the bookies. They update prices the way the house plays blackjack in a casino, sticking to fixed rules. This avoids monstrous blunders and seems to yield steady profits over time. But they take little note of when a game turns, and give little credit for a team threatening to sneak an equaliser. At 1.5, you are being offered roughly 7–1 on a draw, and nearly 17–1 on a victory. If you can pick your moments, there is good money to be made. This is not quite as easy as it sounds, of course. You will lose more often than you win. But the losses should be small. The winnings, if you are judicious, will be big.

Although goals are far harder to come by than we often think, they are most likely at the end of a match. One in six goals, or 17 per cent, come after the 79th minute. This is partly because of the presence of injury-time, which usually runs to three or more minutes. People often downplay the importance of injury-time. Commentators add to the confusion. When the game clock reaches the 85th minute they will say there is 'just five minutes left to play', when there are really seven or eight minutes left. Far more goals are scored in the '90th' minute, which includes injury-time, than in any other.

Further boosting the tally of late goals are the dynamics of close games. Teams trailing by a goal throw caution to the winds as the clock runs down in a desperate bid to level the score. Teams in the lead take advantage by scoring, when possible, on the break. And, of course, players tire as the game goes on. They may lose their concentration and make mistakes. It all adds up.

If you take a punt at 1.5 at £10 a point and it doesn't come off, you have lost just £15. One equaliser will make up for five losses. Oh, and it's fun. The chance – or hope – of making £85 can even make the final fifteen minutes of a dull Nationwide League match interesting. The Win Index usually relates to the result after 90 minutes only, and if a game goes to extra time or penalties both sides make up at 10. This is worth checking before you bet.

If you think a team will not only win but win well, you might chance your arm buying it in the Team Performance market. Equally, if you predict a dire performance you might look to sell. Team Performance is a great idea, but it has two big problems. The first is that it is a purely artificial market and is difficult to track values over a long period of time. The second is that the main bookies cannot agree among themselves exactly how the market should be made up. They measure slightly different factors, and weight them differently.

Sporting Index's market might be called Win Index Plus. It awards 25 points for a win and 10 for a draw, but also gives extra credit for goals (15 points), keeping a clean sheet (10 points) and corners won (3 apiece), while subtracting points for bookings (take off 5 points for each yellow card and 15 for a red). It also gives 10 points if a shot on goal hits the woodwork, but only if the ball rebounds into play.

The market is dependent on so many factors that it is hard to pin down where the prices ought to start. The best approach in these situations is to imagine some reasonable base-case scenarios. A premiership team that wins 2–1 would on average collect around 60 points – 25 for the win, 30 for the two goals, 15 for a typical five corners, less 10 for two cards. But this will vary. Adding an extra three corners would produce a make-up of 69. Four yellow cards instead of two would make it 50. If a team wins 2–0, again winning five corners and collecting two yellows, the result would include an extra 10 for a clean sheet, making up at 70. Cantor and Spreadex offer similar Team Performance markets, with some variations. IG's market is more whimsical. It gives you one point for every minute your team keeps a clean sheet, and subtracts 10 points for every goal conceded. So although other factors are involved – goals scored, corners won and bookings – this becomes in effect a bet on whether your team will keep a clean sheet.

Naturally the strength of the defence, the skill of the goalkeeper and the danger posed by the opposing attack all play their part. So too does home-field advantage. In England home teams keep a clean sheet one-third of the time. The figure varies little, from 35 per cent in the Premiership to 33 per cent in Division Three. On the road this drops to 23 per cent, or in just under one game in four.

This market is highly volatile, and can easily turn on a fluke. Imagine a team that ekes out a dull 1–1 draw, winning an average five corners and getting two bookings. Its Team Performance at Sporting would be 30 (10 points for the draw, plus 15 for the goal scored, plus 15 for the corners, less 10 for the bookings). But the same market at IG would make up anywhere between 10 and 100, depending on when the team conceded the goal.

Juventus are at home to Arsenal in a curious, almost moot Champions League match. The Italians are out. They cannot qualify for the next round. The Gunners can, but that depends on what happens in the night's other group match, between Deportivo La Coruña and Bayer Leverkusen.

Juventus have their minds on Serie A, where they are still title contenders. A big match looms at the weekend. As this match is pointless for them, they are resting most of their big players. Strikers Allesandro Del Piero, David Trezeguet and Marcelo Salas are on the bench. So are key players Igor Tudor and Pavel Nedved, and the goalkeeper Gianluigi Buffon. The defence is shot through with injuries. Paolo Montero and Lilian Thuram are out. Ciro Ferrara is suspended. This is the B-team. The pair tipped to open as strikers have yet to score a league goal between them. The team will not even benefit from the usual home-field advantage. Most local fans have lost interest in a pointless match. The Delle Alpi Stadium, says both the *Racing Post* and the *Evening Standard*, will be half empty.

Meanwhile, Arsenal are going all out. Thierry Henry, still serving a domestic suspension, is rested and ready.

Robert Pires is in form. Ashley Cole, while recovering after several weeks' injury, is on the bench and ready to come on if needed.

Juventus are most likely either to lose or draw. This makes them a tempting sell in Team Performance, where Sporting have priced them at 38 to sell, 42 to buy. The possibilities are attractive. If Juventus lose 1–0, they will get just 3 points for every corner, less 5 points for every yellow card. If you reckon on five corners and two yellows, they will make up at just 5. If they draw 1–1, they will get 10 points for the draw, 10 points for the goal, plus the 5 points mentioned above. That would be 25, still a clear profit if you sold at 38. If they draw 0–0, they will get 10 points for the draw, 10 points for keeping a clean sheet, plus the 5. That would also be 25. To top 38 they probably have to keep a clean sheet and win. This is certainly possible, but seems unlikely. The killer is that Arsenal and Juventus's Team Performance prices are nearly level. Surely the Arsenal As deserve a better rating than the Juventus Bs, even when playing in Italy. Others have the same opinion. By the time you place your order Juve's price has dropped to 36. You sell.

Matters become very clear as the first half unfolds. The B team are up for the match. They have something to prove. They are, if anything, getting the better of the game. Worse, Bayer Leverkusen take the lead in the other group match. If that stands it will make an Arsenal victory as pointless as a Juventus one. The teams will get the news at the break, if they do not already know. At half-time Arsenal and Juventus are 0–0. The only players now with an interest in the game are those Juventus reserves hoping to make an impression.

You can deal at the break. Team Performance is not traded in the running, only before kick-off and at half-time. Sporting, unbelievably, quote 16–19. They tell me Juventus's performance currently stands at 'minus 5', because one player has been booked and the team has won no corners. But that ignores the 20 points they are also on track to win, 10 for the clean sheet and 10 for the draw. You are being offered a quick 17-point profit. Take it. You buy back at 19.

In the second half Bayer Leverkusen widen their lead to two goals, making this game irrelevant. Juventus score off a corner, and Arsenal lose heart. Thierry Henry misses a penalty, his second in recent weeks. Juventus also collect a bagful of corners, and they win 1–0, making up in the mid-40s. Getting out for a profit was a good move.

The popularity of betting on results has thrown out a wide variety of other markets. Certs, offered by Sporting, is an old-fashioned accumulator converted into an index. The bookie nominates three teams due to play on a given day. If all three win, they will give you 50 points. Otherwise the result is zero. For each nominated team which gets four or more goals, they will give you another 10 points.

Spread firms offer these for two reasons. The first is that many in the industry came from the fixed odds business. The second is that punters love them and they are profitable for the bookies. Why? One of the commonest mistakes by amateur gamblers is to overestimate the chances on an accumulator. We can easily imagine those three teams winning. The potential upside is huge. Why should it be so difficult in practice? We tend to add together the chances of each victory, instead of multiplying them. In a six-horse race, the chance of our horse winning (all other things being equal) is one-sixth, or 17 per cent. In three such races we tend to assume, somewhere on the borderline with the subconscious, the chance of our three horses winning is three times that, or 50 per cent. Of course, the real probability of that occurring is less than half a per cent. You have to multiply the chances of the three long shots by each other.

So it is with football. On a typical Saturday, the bookies nominate Arsenal to win at home against Fulham, Liverpool to win at home to Everton in a local derby, and Southampton to win at home to Bolton. The price is 14 to sell, 17 to buy.

You might bet on each individual team to win, but collectively they make a tall order. There is, of course, no perfect way of predicting the outcome of a football match. If there were this book would be a lot shorter, and I would be writing it on a yacht. Attempts to predict results using complicated mathematical formulae, derived from the two sides' goal-scoring patterns, have produced mixed results. But in this case we do not need to predict a result, we need to predict three. This makes the task easier. If we assume that, overall, teams will remain true to form for the season so far we can make a stab at it. Arsenal, so far, have won just five of their twelve Premiership fixtures at home, drawing four and losing three. This suggests their chance of a home victory is just 42 per cent. Fulham, their opponents, have only lost five of twelve away fixtures, winning two and drawing five. Their chance of losing, at least on the record to date, is also 42 per cent. In the second game Liverpool are 6–4–2 at Anfield, a 50 per cent winning record. Everton have lost six of twelve fixtures away, a 50 per cent chance of losing. In the third match Southampton have won five of twelve home matches, a 42 per cent winning record, while Bolton have lost five away, a 39 per cent chance of losing. Multiply these together and you get a measly 8.4 per cent chance that all three teams will win. The correct value of that bet is therefore 8.4 per cent of 50. As 50 is half 100, you can simply halve the percentage to get the value, which is 4.2. It should be even lower than that, because Liverpool are playing Everton. Home-field advantage tends to count for less in a local derby.

The extra points offered for teams scoring four goals adds about 3 points to the value. Teams score four or more in just 11 per cent of Premiership games, and 9 per cent of those in lower divisions. Teams playing at home do so 8 per cent of the time in the Premiership, those playing away less than 3 per cent (the figures in lower divisions are 7 per cent and 2 per cent). Multiply those by 10 points, the prize when it happens, and it adds 0.6 to 0.8 points per game, or less than 3 points for a Certs bet. Adding 3, to be conservative, brings the total value of the particular accumulator to 7.2, or almost exactly half the price. You sell at 14.

Only one of the three teams wins. Liverpool draw 1–1 with Everton and Southampton 0–0 against Bolton. But Arsenal crush Fulham 4–1 at Highbury, Henry scoring twice, Lauren once and Patrick Vieira once. The market makes up at 10, a small 4-point profit.

Sporting also offers Certs for the other three English divisions, on cup nights and weekends, and for overseas competitions. In the Champions League Real Madrid are at home to Porto, Sparta Praha at home to Panathinaikos, and Juventus at home to Deportivo. The bookmaker nominates the three home sides. Domestic form is not going to provide a guide as the Champions League is a case apart. History suggests the correct price should be 6.25. An analysis of the final group stage of the Champions League over the past four years shows that the home team wins 51 per cent of the time, the away team 21 per cent, and the other 28 per cent are drawn. The likelihood of all three home teams winning is 0.5 x 0.5 x 0.5, or 12.5 per cent. Multiply 12.5 per cent by 50 and you get 6.25. At this level, teams score four goals or more rarely. If the bookies are relying on it for their profits, they are in deep trouble. Certs on this night are priced at 13 to sell, 16 to buy. This is easy. There is a clear gap. Sell the Certs at 13.

Sparta lose to the Athenians, as it were, and Juventus are held to a draw by Deportivo in a wild match which sees blown chances and even a missed penalty. So although Madrid defeat Porto 1–0, the market makes up at zero and you collect 13 points profit. No one scored four goals.

The bookmakers made money on Certs – for a while. Amateurs like accumulators, and bought. Then the professionals, who do the numbers, moved in and began taking the value off the table. Sporting began to tighten up, by cutting prices and nominating stronger teams. Later in the 2002 season it ceased to be possible simply to sell the market over and over. On Certs, profits from every three or four winning shorts will be wiped out by a single occasion when the three teams win. You need to be more selective. Look for bets where there are reasonable chances of a draw on all three games. Even one near-certain victory destroys the value. It leaves you betting against two teams instead of three. Certs where some of the nominated teams are playing away are often the best value to sell.

Markets on multiple outcomes come in many forms. Winning Distances offers a chance to bet on teams likely to win away from home on any given Saturday. Sporting measures the distance the teams have to travel and lists them on the website. For an exercise in futility I looked at these one cold, rainy Saturday in March and did some calculations on the back of a very big envelope. Sunderland were travelling 265 miles to Highbury, Villa

102 miles to Bolton, Derby 128 miles to Chelsea, Blackburn 110 miles to Leicester, Charlton 216 miles to Liverpool, Fulham 74 miles to Southampton, and Ipswich 76 miles to West Ham.

The price is 160 to sell, 180 to buy. At first blush, selling would seem crazy. Overall, the teams on the road are travelling 971 miles, or an average of 139 per team. But Sunderland, Derby, Charlton and Ipswich are highly unlikely to win – to put it mildly. Making Sunderland travel 265 miles for a ritual slaughter in north London seems especially cruel. This leaves three possibles: Villa, Blackburn and Fulham. Together these teams are travelling 286 miles. That suggests selling at 160 is not as crazy as first appeared. This market is designed for gambling addicts, the sort who bet on which raindrop will run down a window faster. You can do it if you like, but I wouldn't touch it with a Railtrack timetable.

Not one of the visiting teams won. Arsenal crushed Sunderland 3–0, Bolton beat Villa 3–2, Chelsea beat Derby 2–1, Blackburn lost 2–1 at Leicester, Liverpool beat Charlton 2–0, Southampton and Fulham drew 1–1, and Ipswich lost 3–1 to West Ham. Winning Distances made up at zero.

There is a suspicion this sort of market is usually overpriced. The potential for a big make-up attracts punters dreaming of huge profits, and deters those afraid of big losses. Gimmick markets also mainly attract amateurs just looking for a fun bet, and they are buyers by nature. It's often worth looking at these markets for selling opportunities.

Veteran gamblers on sport in Britain argue strong favourites are generally overfancied in any given match. Amateur punters pile in, sending the price rocketing. You can often find value by going against the trend. The spread firms, noticeably, make money when the favourites fail to live up to their billing – and over the long run the spread firms are making profits. It is always risky backing a heavy favourite away from home. The big-name teams, particularly Man U, Arsenal and Liverpool in England and Real Madrid, Bayern Munich and Roma on the continent, are usually fully priced or even overpriced. As most spread punters are still British, teams well followed here are most likely to attract a heavy weight of money. One of the key figures who developed sports spread betting, market-maker David Garbacz, argues Manchester United in particular are usually overpriced: 'Bookies will give Arsenal 1.6–1.9 at home, and United 1.5–1.8 away. That's a crazy price, but it's up there because the firms know people will buy. The bias in favour of England is smaller than for United.' As usual, the really big return is likelier to come from finding dark horses that are better than people expect.

In international football, however, England are not always overfancied. Sometimes they are underpriced. The English veer wildly between proclaiming their team the greatest in the world, for example after beating Germany 5–1, and denouncing it as the worst collection of football no-hopers in the Western Hemisphere. The truth, generally, is rather more mundane. The English team is usually within the top half-dozen teams in the world. Not once in my lifetime has it been the best, and only very rarely has it been outside the top ten. But the extremes of national manic depression go on.

One veteran spreads follower, gambling journalist and writer Geoff Harvey, argues that, as a result, the English tend to underestimate their chances against strong foreign teams, but overestimate their chances against others. We write the team off before playing Argentina, but expect to beat Poland 9–0. The spreads attract a huge weight of money before England games. It's worth looking for opportunities to bet on a draw by selling the national team when it plays other second-string countries. 'Your clever punters are the ones who oppose the weight of money. They know the price is wrong,' says Patrick Burns, a market-maker at IG Index. Days after trouncing Germany 5–1, England were due to play Albania. Patriotic money poured on to England in the Supremacy market, pushing up the price. 'England fans wanted to pay anything to be with England. They expected to see England win 6–0, 7–0. The clever ones said, "Let's not get carried away here."' England won 2–0. The bookmakers cleaned up, but so did gamblers who kept their heads.

Supremacy was one of the two original football markets in spread betting, and remains among the most popular. The equivalent is also offered for every other sport. In cricket the biggest market is in winning runs, in rugby the winning margin in points. In some there are pitfalls for the unwary. In the World Snooker Championships, for example, Sporting's 'Supremacy' for each match offers 10 points to the player who wins, and 3 for every frame he wins by. You need to check the definition before taking a bet.

Rivalling Supremacy in popularity are the markets on totals – total runs in cricket, total points in rugby and the total number of goals in a football game. Here punters don't care who wins – as long as there are fireworks.

3

Trading Goals

Arsenal are at home to Manchester United on a cold winter afternoon when north London is being battered by driving rain. Walking down Upper Street in Islington, trying to hail a cab, I am getting drenched. The rain is running down the back of my neck and soaking my shirt. Every taxi that passes is occupied. Seeing a bus shelter up ahead I run towards it. I need to get out of the rain so I can use my mobile without getting it wet. There are only a few minutes to kick-off, and I want to deal.

The match is critical. Manchester United have had a weak run recently, losing to Bolton and Liverpool as well as drawing at Old Trafford against Leeds, and their title defence is starting to look wobbly. Arsenal also have a lot to prove today. United have pipped them for the championship three times in three seasons, and memories remain fresh of the last time the two teams met, when United trounced the north Londoners 6–1 at Old Trafford. While Arsenal's bitter historic rivalry is of course with the neighbouring Tottenham Hotspur, in recent times the more important battle has been with Manchester United.

Expect a lively match, despite the rain. The two teams

are big scorers. They also let in plenty of goals. And one interesting fact has emerged from some pre-match research: both teams score and concede goals late in their games. In the past twelve games Arsenal have scored no fewer than nine goals in the final quarter of an hour. Most of the goals they concede are between the 30th and 60th minutes. Man U score even more, but are also weaker at the back. Again, the activity comes well into the game: so far they have scored twenty goals in the second half, and conceded fifteen in the final hour. I want to bet on this.

Among their many markets, the spread betting firms offer a 'Total Goal Minutes'. This adds up the time of each goal in the match, regardless of who scored it. So if a game has one goal scored in minute 20, and one in minute 60, the make-up is 80. If it has three in the 90th minute, the make up is 270. If there is no score, the make-up is zero. Today, the price at kick-off is 150 to buy. This is expensive: at these levels you need at least two late goals to make a profit. Nevertheless, I follow my instincts and buy at 150, at a tiny £1 a point. If there are two goals in the 90th minute, the market will make up at 180 and I will make £30. If there is no score, I lose £150.

Paul Scholes, ominously, opens for Man U in just the 14th minute. This is bad news for the Gooners, but should raise the stakes and so, I hope, the chances of counter-attack. But Arsenal do not reply by half-time. At the break I am still £136 out of the money. However, it's early days. When betting on Total Goal Minutes the second half is where you make your profits.

Three minutes after the break, the marvellous, punk-haired Freddie Ljungberg levels the game for Arsenal. The goal is timed in the 48th minute. Add that to Scholes's goal and Total Goal Minutes now stands at 62, with more than forty minutes to go. Things are looking up. Kanu misses a golden chance, but the Gunners press forward in attack, stretching the Man U defence. It holds, and time ticks away. With barely fifteen minutes left, as the sky darkens and the rain drives hard, the Gunners seem to have run out of steam without anything more to show for it. As I bought at 150, I am still £88 out of the money and am growing increasingly anxious when Fabien Barthez, United's bizarre, Quentin Tarantino-style goalkeeper, takes a simple kick and hoofs the ball straight to Thierry Henry, who capitalises on the mistake and scores. It is a miraculous lifeline, and puts Arsenal 2–1 ahead. Just as importantly, the goal came in the 80th minute. Total Goal Minutes has jumped to 142, leaving me just £8 out of the money. I am still celebrating my escape from a nasty loss when, a few minutes later, United's Reservoir Dog blunders again, trying to handle the wet ball and letting it slip through his hands. Again Henry seizes his chance, giving Arsenal a 3–1 lead with just five minutes left on the clock. A wonderful comeback – and a profitable one for me. The goal is timed at the 85th minute. Add that to the tally, and the TGM is now 227, so I am looking at £77 profit. Greedily, I demand a fifth goal in the dying moments. In a tough battle to the last both teams try to oblige, but the game ends 3–1.

Goals come later than you might expect. The average goal time is around the 50th minute, not the 45th. This is an important figure. Just under 45 per cent of goals come in the first half, and just over 55 per cent in the second. Skewing the results even more is the presence of injury-time. From the point of view of the bookmakers, anything scored in injury-time at the end of the first half is timed at 45 minutes, and anything in injury-time at the end of the match at 90 minutes. With added time at the end these days typically running at three minutes, the 90th minute produces the most goals of all. As a result nearly 80 per cent of the average Total Goal Minutes come from second-half goals; 29 per cent come after the 79th minute. This is because the second half produces more goals, and, obviously, each one adds many more minutes to the final result.

Three days after scoring an upset win in the FA Cup, and apparently riding high, Middlesbrough have to settle down for a north-eastern derby at home against Sunderland. You believe goals will be hard to come by. Boro have performed poorly overall this season and are battling to escape from the relegation zone. They are more likely to be burdened than buoyed by their FA Cup success. Meanwhile, Sunderland have gone five games without a win. Both teams are well below full strength. Boro are missing a number of key players, including star striker Alen Boksic, while Sunderland's Gavin McCann is struggling with injuries. Boksic's absence is especially important. He is Boro's top scorer this season.

The bookies predict total goals of 2.2 to 2.5. As with the Supremacy market, the bookmakers quote the price in tenths of a goal even though this seems a nonsense. How can you have a tenth, or a half of a goal? But if they quoted a price of 2–3, no one would deal. You would hardly sell at 2, because you would only make money if the game ended with just one goal, or none at all. Letting you sell at 2.2 means you will make a profit, albeit a small one, if there are two goals. Equally, it would be foolish to buy total goals at 3. Very few games produce four or more. But if you can buy at 2.5, you will still make money even if there are three.

In this case, you decide the price at 2.2 to 2.5 is too

high. The form would suggest this game will produce two goals or fewer. You sell at 2.2 at £100 a goal. If there are no goals, you will make £220. If there is one goal, £120, and if there are two, £20, which is that small 0.2 margin multiplied by your stake of £100 a goal. In the event the match runs largely as you expected. Noel Whelan scores for Boro in the 14th minute, but there is no further breakthrough over the following seventy-six and the game ends 1–0. The make-up is 1, and your profit is £120.

We watch football games to see goals. They are the stuff of the game. There are no Throw-in of the Season competitions on TV, no North Bank chants of 'Three corners to the Ars-en-AL'. But goals are rarer than we often think. There are 2.65, on average, per Premiership game. More than half of all games, 52 per cent, end up with two or fewer.

The English tend to think of their top league as the most exciting in football, but in terms of goal counts this is not the case. The Spanish and Italian top leagues produce more goals, and Germany's Bundesliga far more, nearly three a game. These numbers provide a useful guide. If you are expecting a lively, attacking game and you can buy total goals at 2.7, this may prove a profitable trade. If the price is 3.3, obviously, the odds are against you. In fact, if the price is 3.1 to 3.4, you might be better off looking instead at selling, or simply avoiding the bet. Matches rarely live up to their hype. If the team with the stronger attack is playing away, you would expect a duller result and at these prices the market is probably a sell. Nearly three-quarters of games, 73 per cent, end with three goals or fewer.

The bookmakers traditionally set the total goals price too high, knowing they would still attract more buyers than sellers. This has changed in recent years, as professional punters moved in and went short, and the rest of their clientele became more sophisticated. But it is still rare to see a sell price below 2.4, and sometimes it rises to 3.3. When two teams with strong attacks and weak defences square off against each other, the likelihood of a goalfest will already be reflected in the price. If the bookmaker offers you the chance to buy total goals at 3.3, for example, remember that just 27 per cent of games would produce a profit at that price. And the profits are likely to be small. Even if you are right and attack dominates, you are far likelier to see a 3–1 or 2–2 result than anything more. Just 14 per cent of games see more than four goals.

People prefer to buy goals instead of selling them for three simple reasons. The first is optimism. We watch football games to see goals. 'Everyone wants to applaud a goal, or a boundary in cricket, so people tend to buy goals rather than sell them,' says Jonathan Sparke, the inventor of sports spread betting. The second is that gamblers want limited downside and unlimited upside, not the other way around. Selling goals at 2.2 at £100 a goal means the best you can make is a profit of £220. Your losses, on the other hand, might be much bigger. A 4–3 result, however unlikely, will leave you £480 out of the money. The third reason is that buying is much more enjoyable. If you are long of goals, you will spend the entire ninety minutes on the edge of your seat, hoping for the ball to go into the back of the net. If you have sold goals, you will spend the time in dread, cringing and looking away every time the play nears the penalty box. It can be a very unpleasant experience.

So prices tend to favour sellers over buyers, at least to date. Industry guru David Garbacz, the original market-maker, has some interesting, if dangerous, advice. 'If you've sold goals, spare yourself the pain,' he says. 'Don't watch the game. Go out.'

It is common to buy goals, lose money, and afterwards put it down to bad luck. We remember all the missed chances, the headers just wide, the strike rattling the crossbar, the ball headed off the line or tipped over by the keeper. 'There could so easily have been three more goals,' people will reason. But these missed chances are not freakish pieces of bad luck. They are not even unusual. A study of the data compiled by Opta, and available on the website, shows just how common they are. Just one shot in eight produces a goal, and just under one in every four shots on target. Goals do not come easily.

The reasons are obvious. We remember goals, especially spectacular ones, and we remember matches with lots of them. That, after all, is why we watch football. We tend to forget all those easily forgettable 0–0 and 1–0 results. When Kevin Keegan returned to Tyneside with Manchester City for the FA Cup, expectations were high. City and Newcastle were among the most exciting attacking teams in English football. The bookmakers offered total goals at 3.3–3.6, Total Goal Minutes at 170–180, and the Goal Minutes for all goals scored by Alan Shearer at 39–43. Selling all three would have been very profitable. Total goals ended up at 1, Total Goal Minutes at 59, and Shearer at sweet FA. Newcastle's Peruvian midfielder Nolberto Solano, who had not scored for two months, scored the only goal. The bookmakers cleaned up. The 1–0 result was not as surprising as it might seem. Data compiled by the Rothmans Football Yearbook show that two-fifths of all games end 0–0, 1–0 or 1–1.

The average game has 2.65 goals, and the average goal time is 50 minutes, so the average for TGM (in the

Premiership) is 130. In Germany, where games produce more goals, the average would be 145.

The bookmaker's spread in Total Goal Minutes is usually 10 points, which is just under 8 per cent of the average make-up. That compares to a nearly 12 per cent profit margin on Total Goals, where the spread is 0.3 and the average make-up 2.65. This is a good edge to have. However, you pay for it with volatility. TGM will make up at zero if there are no goals at all, which happens in one game in eleven, or 9 per cent of the time. However, a 3–2 match with a late flurry can easily end up in the low three figures. You need steel nerves to go short.

The price for TGM has also traditionally been too high, sometimes, as in the Newcastle–Man City game, pushed up to 180 to buy. One bookmaker admitted to me, with disbelief, 'It's amazing. We keep setting the price higher and higher, and people keep buying it.' Once again professionals are moving in, going short and pushing the price back down.

In the Arsenal match, in the ominous second-half spell before Barthez blundered, I took the chance to hedge myself against potential losses by selling Total Goals. With fewer than twenty minutes to go, the price was still 3.3 to sell, even though there had only been two so far. This was far too high – it would be dangerous to rely on such extraordinary mistakes at this level, and without them the match would have ended 1–1. Nevertheless, this price implied there would be 1.3 more goals. I sold at £30 a goal as a partial hedge. As we were already past the 70th minute, every goal from this moment on would add at least £70 to my TGM bet, but would subtract just £30 from my bet on Total Goals. Had there been no further action, my second bet would have made £39, helping minimise the £88 losses on TGM. In the event, the two goals cost me £21 on my Total Goals bet, leaving £56 clear profit overall. It's a form of insurance.

Crunch time. Liverpool are at home to Roma on a wet, blustery night. The Reds have to win. Even worse, they have to beat the team leading the Italian league by two clear goals in order to qualify for the final rounds of the Champions League.

Liverpool are paying the price for letting Galatasaray off with a 0–0 draw in the Turks' visit to Anfield. They are now bottom of their group. A victory by two goals will still let them through. If they win by just one, they can still qualify – but only if the other group match tonight, between Barcelona and Galatasaray, produces a win for either team. And if Liverpool draw, let alone lose, they are out.

Roma know this. Italian teams are usually thought to travel poorly, and they are doubtless nervous ahead of this game. Sitting back and holding on for a draw has to be a losing proposition for them tonight. Their best strategy has to be to go out and score a quick goal, to silence the Anfield crowd. Liverpool, meanwhile, need a big result, so they are also likely to go all out for the first strike.

This gives a good chance for an early goal. The market here is Time of First Goal. The name is self-explanatory. It is priced tonight at 38 to 41. This market works counter-intuitively, so that if you think there will be an early goal you sell, and if you think there won't be you buy. If you think there will be an early goal you would sell at 38 minutes. If the first goal comes in the 8th minute, you have made a 30-minute profit. If you bet £1 a minute, your profit is £30. If you bet £1,000 a minute, your profit is £30,000. On the other hand, if the first goal does not come until the 90th minute, you will lose 62 minutes, the difference between 38 and 90. If you bet £1 a minute, your losses are £62. If you bet £1,000 a minute, you are in deep trouble.

The average first goal in an English match comes in the 35th minute. The market is usually priced around 34 to sell, 37 to buy. If there is no goal, the market is settled at 90.

Tonight's price, of 38 to sell, looks way too high. Liverpool are the fourth highest goal scorer in the Premiership (52 from 31 games), Roma the fourth highest in Italy (43 from 27). Between them, the two teams score 3.3 a game, or one every 27 minutes. Local results are not wholly applicable to a Champions League match, but they give an indication. Liverpool have not scored in a Champions League match since November, when they lost 3–1 at home to Barcelona. They have faced Galatasaray twice and Roma once in goalless draws. But apart from those, they have tended to score at least one per home game. Critically, there is no point holding back tonight. They have to win this match to go through. A draw will not do it. So they can be expected to throw everything at the Romans.

You sell at 38 at £10 a minute. The match obliges almost better than you could imagine. Both teams attack strongly, and in the opening minutes a scramble in the Roma box produces a penalty. Liverpool's Finnish striker Jari Litmanen, standing in for an injured Michael Owen, slots it away cleanly in the 7th minute. Your profit is 31 minutes, or £310. Nice work. Liverpool go on to win 2–0, and Barcelona edge the Turks 1–0. A good night for England.

There is also a market for the time of the second goal. The price starts much higher, giving you more potential for profit in a big-scoring game. That also means your losses will be smaller if there are no goals, as both markets will make up at 90. But it leaves you at risk from 1–0 victories, and matches where the second goal comes late.

Leeds are at home to West Ham. Leeds and their new striker Robbie Fowler are in form, scoring plenty of goals and remaining in striking distance of the top of the Premiership. On the other hand, they have had problems at the back, putting in some sloppy performances. In the past month they have let in two against Leicester, two against Everton, and four to Newcastle. Nor are West Ham obvious pushovers. In the last month they have beaten Man U at Old Trafford 1–0, drawn 1–1 at home against Liverpool, Arsenal and Aston Villa, and thumped Derby 4–0. They have not lost for seven games – and that was a 1–0 defeat away at Sunderland with the goal coming in the 85th minute.

The price for the Time of First goal is 34 to 37. This could well be a high-scoring game and you might expect Leeds to attack early, especially at home. More attractive is the price for the Time of Second goal, at 57–60 minutes. The six games Leeds have played since Fowler joined them, all in the Premiership, have seen the following numbers of goals: 3, 4, 5, 7, 3, 1. That averages 3.83 goals per game, or one every twenty-three minutes. You sell the time of the second goal at 57 at £5.

The match goes better than you could possibly expect. Leeds are all over the Hammers from the off, Viduka scoring within four minutes – and then again soon afterwards. The time of the second goal? The 7th minute. Your profits are £250 after watching seven minutes of a football game. You take no further interest in the game and head down the pub instead. Leeds eventually win 3–0.

Many bookmakers allow you to trade these markets in running, so you can watch a few minutes of the game before you bet. As time ticks by without a goal, the bookmakers will keep raising the prices. Naturally the best moment to sell is just before a goal, though this requires almost perfect judgment. But on several occasions the ball has gone into the net while I am dialling, which is no use at all. The Time of Second Goal market has an additional advantage. If there is an early first goal, the price for the second will drop sharply: 'As soon as the first goal goes in, we drop the price for the second goal to where it was for the first,' says IG's Gary Hope. If the first strike comes in the first ten minutes, the time for the second goal will usually drop to the low 40s. The profits from a quick exit will be modest, but it does offer a second way to play this market. But not all bookmakers offer this market in running at the moment. Check first.

The goal times markets are so popular that they have spawned an array of cousins – Time of Last Goal, Time of Winning Goal, Time of First Equaliser (a rarity, usually only brought out for cup finals). There are also markets for Time of First Goal by Each Team, in case you have a view on one side or another.

Chelsea are away at Old Trafford. The Blues are looking strong, having lost just one Premiership match this season, while the home side is having a poor run, losing games recently to arch-rivals Arsenal and Liverpool. Since selling their star defender Jaap Stam, their defence has become decidedly ropy. They have let in 13 goals in their last 7 Premiership games. Despite this, the bookies think Chelsea will not score their first goal for 57 to 59 minutes. This looks way too high.

When Chelsea score, they do so early. Although they have scored only 16 goals in 13 games this season, they have scored 12 (nearly 1 per game) inside 60 minutes. Jimmy-Floyd Hasselbaink, who provided most of those, might be the fastest striker in the league as well as, arguably, the best. On average, they score their first goal in the 42nd minute. If you sell, your potential profit (57 minutes) is far higher than your potential loss (33 minutes).

The price is skewed by three recent results when Chelsea failed to score. With United struggling, this does not look like it is going to be the fourth. You sell Chelsea's first goal at 57 at £5. The defender Mario Melchiot obliges by heading the ball in for the Blues in the 6th minute. As you sold at 51 minutes higher than that, with a £5-a-minute stake, your profit is a tasty £255. Hasselbaink doesn't get off the mark until an hour has passed. Chelsea win 3–0.

There are all sorts of ways of playing the goal markets. If you think the first and second goals will come in quick succession you could buy Time of First Goal and sell Time of Second Goal for exactly the same amounts. The two bets partially cancel out each other. You don't care whether the two goals come early in the match or late. As long as the time difference is narrower than the bookies have predicted, you will make money. Those entranced by complexity may be tempted to chance their arm, but there is one good word of advice: KISS, Keep It Simple, Stupid.

Trading goal time markets in running can also provide good opportunities, if you are quick.

It's the 'Game of the Century' – again. In Spain this takes place at least twice a year. Barcelona are at home to Real Madrid. Ordinarily, these two are slugging it out for the top spot in La Liga. This time it has slightly less significance. Real are standing second in the league and need a win to move into first place. Barca are six points behind their old rivals. They need a result to stay in with a chance.

It is business as usual at the Nou Camp. The world's most magnificent football stadium is buzzing, Catalan flags flutter in the wind, smart-looking types are puffing away on cigarettes in the prime seats, and Real Madrid are whistled on to the pitch. When Barca appear, roars emerge and the words FA BARCELONA appear on the far stand as the fans hold their cardboard squares aloft. A marvellous camera shot, from high up at the back of the third gallery, gives even the TV viewer vertigo. You can hardly see the pitch. This is *Ben-Hur* without the chariots. The commentators, for once, are on good form. 'Two of the English towns which were this week declared cities would fit into this stadium,' says one. The Nou Camp holds 95,000 people, a third more than Old Trafford.

European politicians are in town for some EU jolly. None seems to have made the game, which says a great deal. How can you call yourself a 'European leader' and turn down free tickets for this? A side-effect is that the leaders and their camp followers have occupied the main hotels in town. Real Madrid – whose best player, Zinedine Zidane, is worth more than most European parliaments – were forced to put up at a second-choice hotel on the outskirts. The footballing talent on display tonight is a marvel. 'Welcome to the real European Summit,' remarks a commentator.

Most of the markets seem reasonably priced. Time of First Goal is 35 to sell, 38 to buy. This becomes significant within moments.

Two minutes after kick-off, three morons rush on to the pitch to protest for or against something or other. They might be 'anti-capitalist' protesters, but there are no expensive laptops or mobile phones visible so perhaps not. Or they might be Catalan or Basque nationalists. They are unlikely to win any friends among the 95,000 Catalans in the stands. Either way, they handcuff themselves to the goals. This is your chance.

The police and stewards immediately gather round and

look baffled. Someone is sent to get skeleton keys. Someone else is dispatched to get a hacksaw. The goals might have to be lifted. We are looking at a significant delay of the game. Yet in the top right-hand corner of your TV screen, the game clock ticks on.

You can immediately buy Time of First Goal at 38 minutes. There will be no goals while the idiots are removed. It is reasonable to assume, too, that the match, even when it restarts, will take several minutes to get going again properly. The players came on to the pitch fired up. Now they are idly kicking balls around and chatting to one another.

In this circumstance you would bet heavily, £100 a minute or more. You have to move quickly, because the bookmakers who offer this market in running will suspend trading when they see the delay is going to be significant. It takes a good five minutes to remove the protesters, who are then led away with a police escort rather than, as some might prefer, handed over to the crowd for instant justice. Play resumes.

Time of First Goal has now risen to 40 to 43. Because this market enjoys a reasonably small, three-minutes spread, you are already able to trade back out at a profit. You bought at 38. Now you can sell at 40. Markets with fat spreads are virtually useless for in-the-running trades because even when they move it might not be enough to cover the bookmaker's margin. Selling ToFG now is tempting, as you were only taking advantage of the delay. However, it is certainly worth holding on for a few minutes more, as the price rises. But get out sooner rather than later.

As predicted, some of the steam has gone out of the match. There is plenty of midfield play but it seems desultory and for a while there are no serious chances. Both

defences look solid. Although many argue you should run
your profits, greed can be the enemy of gain and there are
times to collect what you have. By the half-hour point the
price has risen to 56 to sell, a clear 18 points profit. You
were only betting on a long delay and a slow restart, not
on a goalless draw over ninety minutes. There are goals
in this game, sooner or later. Take the money and run.
Nine minutes later Zinedine Zidane dances through an
opening that did not exist to put Real ahead. Buying at
38 produced a 1-point profit if you held on, and 18 points
if you traded out. The match goes on to finish 1–1, as
Barca fluke an equaliser in the second half. But you
already have your money.

Villa are at home to bottom-place Ipswich, who have won
just 9 points from 16 games. It would be wrong to say
there was much interest, except from devoted fans of the
two clubs. Aston Villa are favoured to win. The Supremacy
price is over 1 (1.1 to buy), which is deeply unappealing.
More than anything, this is likely to be a dull game. Both
teams have weak attacks – Villa have scored an average
of 1.3 goals a game at home, and Ipswich have done
exactly the same away. Both teams are well behaved,
collecting barely one yellow card per game each. Neither
gets many corners. This game could easily end 0–0 after
a dull, miserable ninety minutes. For those making the
trek to Villa Park, only the cold and damp will keep them
awake.

There is a market for this: Match Performance. It should
really be called Dull/Interesting. If the goals, cards, penalties and corners fly, look for a big total. Match
Performance is an invented market, and it varies from
spread firm to spread firm. At IG they give 10 points for
each goal scored, another 10 for each penalty and 10 for

each red card. They also give 3 points for every yellow card and 3 points for every corner. As a kicker, if the match ends 0–0 they deduct 25 points. It cannot be traded in running.

For Villa against Ipswich, IG are quoting a price of 60 to 64 (this later drops to 58 to 62 shortly before kick-off). This looks too high. It would require, say, two open-play goals (20 points), ten corners (30) and three yellows (9). This sounds about as exciting as it might get. Meanwhile, anything less would produce a significantly lower make-up. Imagine some scenarios. A 1–0 match, again with ten corners and three yellow cards, would make up at 49. A 0–0 draw, by no means impossible, would benefit from that 25-point deduction. Even with ten corners and three yellows, it would make up at just 14. One match in eleven ends goalless. Rough calculations suggest an average price of 35 in this market if there are three goals or fewer. You sell at 58 at £10.

The match proves rather livelier than you expect. Ipswich, amazingly, took control early in the match and went into the lead thanks to a deflected strike by Finidi George. Both sides attacked energetically. Villa equalised late in the first half, from a header by Juan Pablo Angel. In the second they went ahead when Angel scored again, and Ipswich looked in danger of crumbling, but they hung on without further loss. The game ended 2–1.

This was not the worst-case scenario, but it was far more interesting than you expected. But because you bet with a good margin of safety, you still made a profit. Although there were more goals than you expected, there were fewer corners (just five) and fewer bookings (one). The make-up was just 48. You still made a 10-point profit, or £100 at £10 a point.

Most money still goes into the basic markets of

Supremacy and Total Goals, but in recent years this has started to change. Goals are rare, and more random than the TV commentators would have you think. A bad bounce, a ball striking the woodwork, a reliable keeper for once caught off his line – a few seconds can decide a match, even against the run of play. The TV pundits always like to pretend afterwards that the result was virtually inevitable, but plenty of 1–0 games could have ended instead as draws, or even gone the other way. Statistics say it takes eight shots on average to produce a goal, including 3.6 on target. But sometimes it takes thirty, and at other times only one. Attention has instead been turning to more incremental markets, which depend on more frequent events, such as the number of corners and bookings.

4

On the Cards

No one in his right mind would bet on a clean Old Firm game. The Glasgow derby has the reputation as the dirtiest match-up in football. But as a result, one afternoon shortly before kick-off the price in the Bookings market is 72 to 74.

Spread firms give 10 points for every yellow card handed out, and 25 points for every sending off. A price in the low 70s is very high – it means the bookies are predicting at least seven yellows, or, say, five yellows and one red. That would be a brutal match. Most British matches at the top level start with a price between 30 and 50. The average make-up in England is 35, and in Scotland – contrary to opinion south of the border – it is no higher.

The best profits come from knowing when to go against the crowd. Some Old Firm matches are still spectacular blowouts, but the days are long gone when eleven Catholics from one side of the tracks lined up against eleven Protestants from the other. Most of the players are from the other side of the North Sea. Just four Scotsmen start this game – two for Rangers (Maurice Ross and Barry

Ferguson), two for Celtic (Robert Douglas and Paul Lambert). Most of the Protestants on the pitch are Scandinavian. The Catholics are Italian.

Even better, the referee for this match – Stuart Dougal, who I think we can assume from his name is Scottish – is relaxed with the cards. In his last six games he handed out five yellows, three yellows and a red, no cards, three yellows, two yellows, and four yellows. In spread betting terms his average is just under 33. This is marginally below the norm.

You sell at 72. Keeping it conservative you bet just £2 a point. Alas, south of the border the Old Firm game can only be viewed on pay per view, even though it is the only Scottish football match worth watching. This is yet another example of how stupid it is to keep two of the best teams in Britain caged up in a tiny, segregated market where their only real opposition is each other. The Scots will doubtless object, but I would much rather see Celtic play Liverpool twice a year than Hibernian four times. So, I suspect, would many Celtic fans, although I wouldn't expect a single one to admit it.

So if you are one of the 55 million people in Britain who does not live in Scotland, you simply have to place a bet on this match and hope for the best. Checking the result online later shows there were five bookings. Two Celtic players – Hartson and Moravcik – and three from Rangers – Ball, Ferguson and Konterman – get cautioned. There are no reds. Bookings makes up at 50. As you sold at 72 at £2 a point, your profits are £44.

Perhaps, in general, we want to see a bloodbath. Perhaps the occasional appallingly badly behaved games are so memorable we assume they happen more often than they do. Or perhaps we assume the players are as prone to thuggery as some of the fans are. For whatever reason, the

Bookings market offers good opportunities to make easy money by going short. The price, at least in recent years, has generally been set too high. Professional punters made good money by selling Bookings before every match.

Things are getting tougher. As more professionals make this bet, the bookies have dropped their prices. You need to be more selective, but the bookmakers know people are still reluctant to sell, for the usual reasons. You would rather spend the match in hope than in fear. And the potential profits from selling are limited, while the risk is unknown. In practical terms, what is the worst that is likely to happen?

In very recent times the Old Firm did set the record. In 2001 the Glasgow derby saw three red cards and ten yellows, making up at an astonishing 175 points. In 1999 the two teams reached nearly that level, making up at 165. These are, of course, exceptions. When Germany met Cameroon in the 2002 World Cup, there were fourteen yellow cards and two reds, making up at 190. Punters won, and bookmakers lost, several hundred thousand pounds. Some friends in the City, who like to go short of bookings, had a serious sense of humour failure. Overall, the average for the past six seasons has been 70, but that gives hefty weight to the occasional blowouts. Half the games made up at 55 or less. Nearly three-quarters, 72 per cent, made up at 60 or below.

In the Premiership in the 2001–2 season the record was set early on when Arsenal faced Leeds. Nine players were cautioned and two were sent off. The market made up at 140. These days such results are rare. Last season just 1 per cent of Premiership games saw Bookings make up over 100 points. Two of those involved Leeds. While intense rivalries live on among the fans, modern players at the top of the game are apt to be more concerned about their bankability, winning product endorsements, avoiding serious injury and perhaps getting a chance to play on the world stage for their countries. These are not things that encourage you to risk limb and suspension on a rash tackle. It is more remarkable that many still do.

The average in England in recent years is 35 points per game – halfway between three and four yellows, or the equivalent to a yellow and a red. But that includes a few big bloodbaths. Two-fifths of games see two yellows or fewer. If you sell at 35 before every game you would make money 57 per cent of the time, although the few blowouts would wipe out your profits. You will get the best value if you wait for Bookings prices well above that.

Bookings are more reliable in league games. When teams stray outside for other competitions, such as the FA Cup, they come up against players used to different standards. Referees also struggle to impose one of set rules on players from different levels. That can make the number of cautions and sendings-off less predictable. Also, players have an additional incentive not to behave stupidly or dangerously when playing within their own league: they will have to meet the same team again very soon. They may even be offered a lot of money to join it.

For players, the referee's whistle for a foul is often frustrating, and yellow cards infuriating. But red cards are sobering: one of their own has been sent off, they have to settle down to a different game. They also, I suspect, wonder if they might be next. The best time of all to sell Bookings is when there is a fist fight on the pitch. The price will be soaring as traders bet on a lot more blood. But once it is over the players are likely to simmer down, their anger spent.

Even games that turn dirty rarely turn *too* dirty. Of games where the Bookings index hits 50 points – equal to five yellow cards, or two reds – most, 57 per cent, finish with either no more cards, or just one, to make up at 60 or less. Fourth-fifths make up below 80. Just 5 per cent of games where the Bookings count hits 50 go on to reach 100. (See Appendices, Table 14.)

Bayer Leverkusen are at home to Dortmund in what is virtually a local derby, as well as a battle for the top of the German Bundesliga. There is little goodwill between the clubs and the bookies set prices of around 60 for Bookings before the match. This offers no opportunity to buy, but little to sell before the game.

The fouls come thick and fast early on. Dortmund's ill-humour is worsened when a goal is disallowed for a dubious offside. The first yellow card comes early, and they continue to be awarded regularly on both sides. Shortly before half-time there is a huge row at the Dortmund goal, where the keeper, Jens Lehmann, and Leverkusen striker Ulf Kirsten both scrambled for the ball and came into sharp contact. They start jostling each other and the two sides pour in to pull them apart. Both players get carded. At half-time the count is 60, and the price has risen to 96 to 99. It looks tempting, but it is still too soon to sell. Five players are on cautions, leaving open a significant possibility of a red. The game is still tight at 1–0, so both sides will continue to fight hard for the ball. But a red card will be a selling opportunity. Three minutes into the second half the Dortmund captain, Jan Koller, is cautioned for a sloppy tackle. Moments later the Dortmund defence, looking half asleep, defends lazily against a corner and Carsten Ramelow taps the ball in for 2–0. In his frustration, three minutes later Koller kicks out in defence in a late challenge and the referee flourishes a second yellow. The captain is sent off.

At this moment the price on Bookings soars as traders'

emotions get the better of them. The price goes as high as 108. Yet the game is essentially over. Leverkusen are 2–0 up at home and Dortmund are down to ten men. There is nothing to play for except dignity, and there is barely half an hour left of the match. Even with the red card, Bookings so far only total 85. The market is pricing in another red as the most likely outcome when it is surely a worst-case scenario. In England only half of games that get to 85 points on Bookings even reach 100. This looks a clear sell – and indeed so it proves, the final price for Bookings making up at 85. Leverkusen also tapped in two more goals to make the result 4–0.

To prove the irrationality of the market at heated moments, fifteen minutes after the red card, when there had been no further cautions, the price for bookings stood at 98 to 101. There were barely twenty minutes to play and the score was 3–0.

If you are minded to sell Bookings, there are two good times to do it. The first is during the first ten minutes of the game, if you have seen evidence that this is likely to be a much friendlier game than the market had expected. The bookmakers do not tend to start reducing the price until the 10th minute. The second is after a card, if it is a fluke during an otherwise good-natured game. Bookings for dissent, and technical red cards for a last-man foul on a striker running at the goal often come into this category.

The TV coverage is not always helpful. When a player earns a yellow card for a foul, they immediately replay the tackle from different angles, while pundits argue about whether he got the ball, went for the ball, and so on. Those who want to sound posh call a rash tackle 'naïve'. What you really want to watch, though, is not what happened just before the tackle but what happens immediately after-wards. Football players do not usually hate one another as much as their respective fans do, and even bad tackles are often to some extent inadvertent. Frequently the offender helps up his victim and (sometimes) even apologises. At this moment the price on Bookings has jumped, and it can be a good chance to sell.

When Man City played Newcastle, the FA Cup tie featured two teams with clean records. The referee, Alan Wiley, had handed out just one red card in his previous twenty-four games. His average Bookings make-up was just 29. In the first half-hour City defender Richard Dunne was sent off for a last-man foul and the Bookings price jumped to 46 to sell. Yet there were few tough tackles, and even Dunne's offence had amounted to little more than shirt pulling. Bookings were a clear sell. Shearer collected a yellow in the second half, but that was it. The market made up at 35, a good 11-point profit.

It is often assumed in Britain that continental games see many more bookings. In some leagues, such as the Bundesliga, this is not the case, but in others it is. In Spain's La Liga, the average make-up is a horrendous 60. The English equivalent would be if every match featured Arsenal playing itself, with Ray Parlour sliding in late to tackle Dennis Bergkamp, and Martin Keown exacting revenge. And these are just the averages. The dirtiest teams in Spain, Alaves and Malaga, average 39 and 37 points a game each. That is higher than the average total for both sides in England.

The best-behaved Spanish teams, including Real Madrid, Barca and Deportivo, collect between 22 and 24 points on average per game – or about the same as the worst-behaved teams in the Premiership.

Italian matches also feature more bookings than those in England, although there is some evidence that the referees are stricter: they allow fewer fouls before showing a card. Two of the worst teams in Italy in 2001/2 hailed from the same town: Chievo Verona (32 points per game) and Verona (30 points). These were comfortably ahead of Arsenal (23 points), and more than twice as bad as Southampton (13, or just over one yellow card). The Verona derby must be a treat. However, Italy's best-behaved team, Juventus, was in Southampton's league, collecting a mere 16 points a game.

The pattern of bookings can also work differently. In Spain there is often a flood of yellow cards in the last ten minutes. Frequently players are booked for dissent, even then. In England referees are reluctant to book in the final ten minutes. Patrick Burns from IG says, 'When I'm not at work, I will often call around the spread firms ten or twelve minutes before the end to see if I can sell Bookings at effectively a point for every minute left. Quite often I can.' He has found this to be profitable.

When trading in Bookings, you aren't just buying or selling the records of the two teams. You are also trading the referee. In a perfect world all refs would hand out exactly the same number of red and yellow cards. They don't. Their records show just how far we still are from consistent refereeing. Most of the regulars in the Premiership end up in a fairly narrow band, but their averages still vary between 30 to 40 Bookings points per game over the season. A few sit well outside this band. In 2001/2 the most card-happy of the regular Premiership refs, Mike Riley, handed out the equivalent of more than five yellow cards per game. In matches he refereed Bookings made up at 55 on average. The most lenient, David Elleray, averaged only 27. A closer look at their records shows just how widely the two differ. Riley, in the course of seventeen games, had just two mild matches. In one the make-up was 20 and in the other it was 10. By contrast he had eight matches over 50 points, including a spectacular 125 (Bolton against Leicester), where he sent off three players and cautioned five. You are unlikely to make much shorting Bookings in his matches. Elleray also refereed one blood-bath, the season opener between Everton and Spurs, which made up at 100, with five cautions and two sendings-off. But of his other sixteen Premiership games, not one saw the Bookings count rise above 50. Four saw two yellows, another four just one, and one, admittedly the last game of the season, saw none at all.

If you have decided to sell, wait. Do not place the bet until a few minutes of the game have passed. Even if there are no fouls, and the match seems particularly good natured, the Bookings price tends to fall very slowly. This favours the patient seller, who waits to see how the match will develop.

Crystal Palace are at home to Wolves. There is talk of a grudge match, and the Bookings price is set a little on the high side, at 40 to 42, before kick-off. But in the tunnel before coming on the two sides can clearly be seen on TV chatting away to one another amicably. The friendly nature of the match is obvious immediately. In the first twenty minutes there are no cards shown, and indeed there isn't even a rough tackle, but you can still sell cards at 36. Shortly before half-time the price is still 28 to 31. When a Wolves player is injured Palace kick the ball out. Afterwards, Wolves return possession by kicking the ball to the Palace goalkeeper, who fumbles and lets the ball bounce out for a corner. A Wolves player runs down to the corner flag and takes the corner – generously kicking the ball straight out again for a goal kick. Bookings by this stage are still priced at 24 to 27, probably too low to sell comfortably, although still very tempting. The final make-up is 20.

When Barcelona hosted Real Madrid last season the Bookings market was priced at 72 to 76 before the off. This is a grudge match, the national derby. But these are also two of the best-behaved teams in Spain. Their averages would suggest a typical make-up around 45. The reason for the high price was the record of the referee, Perez Burrull, who is one of the toughest in Spain. 'He's a complete maniac,' said one market-maker. The Opta website shows that Burrull that season averaged more than five yellow cards a game, and a red every other match. Amazingly this is not enough to make him the toughest ref in Spain, although he is within the top half-dozen.

But you have to take a view. The stands are full of national celebrities. This is a big occasion. Although the game promotes rivalry, the players are likely to be on better behaviour than otherwise. Meanwhile, you suspect Burrull does not want to be the man who ruined the match. A big fiesta-style occasion is likely to see lower Bookings. This is also true, for example, of the FA Cup Final.

Just after kick-off, when the game is delayed for five minutes by protesters, Bookings becomes an even more compelling sell. Although the price has ticked down to 68 the disruption clearly discharges the initial tension. The players relax by kicking balls around. The crowd are suddenly jeering the protesters, not Real. You do not have to take a view of the final outcome. You can simply trade, selling now and buying back when studs start to find ankles again. It is possible to take a view that the price will tick lower for some time after play resumes. Bookings also has a reasonably narrow margin of 4 points, which makes in-running trading easier. In a game where the price is set at 72 to 76 that is just 5.5 per cent. You might need just ten minutes without incident before opportunities emerge to buy it back at a profit.

Selling at 70 proved profitable. The game resumed after the disruption in a desultory fashion and took a while to pick up the tempo. The referee was reluctant to intervene. He played the advantage, and when whistling for a foul ignored frequent appeals for cards. In the 39th minute the game came alive when Zidane put Real Madrid ahead. The crowd in the Nou Camp, already fed up with their team's poor recent performance, became restless and started jeering the home players. Furthermore, the game was entering the danger zone, the last five minutes of the first half, when players' concentration slips and they start making mistakes. This became the moment to buy back Bookings, which had now ticked down all the way to 56 to buy. It was an easy 14-point profit. The first yellow card did not appear until the 51st minute. More came after that as Barca were roundly booed by their own fans and showed signs of desperation. Barcelona's flukey equaliser did not help Real's humour either. The King's team were hoping for their first win at the Nou Camp in nearly two decades. Helped by a late flurry of cards, the final make-up was 80. Buying at 76 would have proved marginally profitable after all. But selling in running did too – if you knew when to get out.

This produced some controversy back in London later. Bookings are so common in Spain that they are not always shown on TV, and in the second half the referee waved two yellow cards which no one outside the stadium saw. This left the bookmakers quoting prices 20 points below the correct level, and people traded on that basis. The firms had to add 20 after the fact to prices and the make-up. If you sold out before the cards started flying it did not affect you. But it is a danger of in-running trading on Bookings in La Liga: 'This happens quite often in Spanish games,' one market-maker admitted. The only way to handle it is to check the current level with the bookmaker when you call to bet. They will usually volunteer the information, because they know very few are keeping track of bookings. This is also the case with the next market, Corners.

5

Corner Kicks

I didn't really mind the money I lost betting on a Real Madrid comeback in the Spanish Cup Final. What infuriated me was the easy profit I missed at the same time. The bet on Real, although a losing one, was a reasonable one. Missing out on an easy bet on Corners was stupid.

Before the start of the match between Real and Deportivo, the price for Total Corners was 10 to 11. This is the standard opening price, and reflects the average number of corners in games. After fifteen minutes, when Deportivo had stunned the Bernabeu by taking an early lead and I was buying Real in the Win Index, the price for Corners was unmoved, still at 10 to sell, 11 to buy.

Yet so far there had been just one. Furthermore, that had not come through the usual source, strong attacking play down the wings. Instead it had come out of the blue, from a surprise shot on goal that Real keeper Sanchez Cesar tipped over the crossbar. Attack continued to be down the centre. This was an easy sell. The price soon caught up with events and began ticking downwards with the clock. Even with a late flurry in the second half it made up at only 7, a good 3-point profit.

You can always tell a spread better, because he knows how many corners there were in a game. Corners markets are among the more popular with gamblers. Teams vary significantly in the number they win and give away. According to the football statistics website, Soccerbase, West Ham conceded nearly 6 a game at home in 2001/2, Arsenal just 2.5; Man U won 8 a game at home, Sunderland just 5. Newcastle and Man U won more than 5 a game on the road, Derby and Middlesbrough fewer than 3. The average team wins 5 a game: reflecting the attacking advantages at home, they will win 6 in their own park, and 4 on the road. 'Most games make up between five and fifteen,' says David Garbacz of Sporting Index. 'The volatility in this market is small.' There have been a few much higher, in the twenties, but these occur rarely, and mostly in the lower leagues. Nevertheless, obviously, corners occur more often than goals. You are therefore less at the mercy of freak events. If a team is strong down the flanks and is going all out on the attack, they might score three goals or they might not, but they are likely to win a lot of corners.

Twice inside a month I stood in the North Bank at Highbury and watched Liverpool's midfielders persistently try to lob the ball down the middle to Michael Owen. The scampering superstar jumps for the ball. So does Arsenal's towering defender Sol Campbell. The only people who think Owen has a chance in these circumstances live on Merseyside and wear track suits to work. Campbell could win the ball without leaving the ground.

These sorts of peculiarities offer some good opportunities for profit. One of the most successful betting strategies for much of the 2001/2 season was to go short of Liverpool corners. They hardly ever played down the wing, and rarely won a corner. For the first half of the season they were winning fewer than four a game – well below the standard for top-flight teams. Later in the season Liverpool began changing their strategy and using the flank more, and the corner count rose.

Accurate data is still hard to get, but market-makers say Spanish games tend to see fewer. The bookies used to make good money on this market simply by setting the price too high. And still the punters piled in. One veteran recalls, 'We used to have one guy, back in the early days, who bought corners before every game. He was something in the City and he had a lot of money, and he would buy Corners at a thousand pounds a point. We kept pushing the price up and he kept buying. We reached a point where we were charging sixteen to buy, and still he would deal. I couldn't believe it. But I guess nobody is that rich. Eventually he stopped dealing.'

The Total Corners market has the great advantage that you can trade it in the running. It is a good professional's market. A game which is looking dull, with desultory midfield action, may produce a freak goal but it is unlikely to produce a freak run of eight corners any time soon. If you spot this trend early you can sell, wait for the price to tick down with the clock, then buy back. You need to be clear about what you are doing. Do not sell at high stakes. That leaves you the possibility of selling more, at an even better level, if there is a sudden flurry of corners. However, in each of those cases you need to be certain that they are against the trend of the game. If the wingers have suddenly come to life at both ends, and three corners come in quick succession, you might have to take your loss and buy your bet back. The longer the time between opening the bet and closing it, the lower your losses.

Corners, like buses, often come in threes. A team has a good spell in attack, keeping up pressure on the defence and forcing flag kicks. Or one corner leads directly to another, as the defenders head the ball out. This does not go on for ever. It is often a good chance to sell. Again, you can buy back later, when things have quietened down. As always with this sort of momentum trading, the trick lies in being quick. You need to sell when you spot the trend, and be ready to take your profits before things move against you.

For many punters, however, the Total Corners market did not offer enough volatility. So the bookies got creative.

Newcastle are away to a resurgent Man U, who have bounced back from the disasters of November to win five in a row. The odds have to be on a big attacking game. Both teams are battling for the lead in a wide-open Premiership race. Man U, with 48 goals from 19 games, are the top scorers in the league. Newcastle, with 38 from 21, are third. But the Magpies are more dangerous on the road, where so far this season they have scored 22 goals in 11 games, than at St James's Park, where they have put in 16 from 10 games. When this pair last met Newcastle won 4–3 thanks to an own goal in the last ten minutes.

The obvious bets are only being offered at unattractive prices. You would have to buy Total Goals at 3.3. The Time for the First Goal is a low 31 to 34 minutes. It is easy to see no breakthrough in the first half-hour. The Second Goal, at 54 to 57 minutes, looks more appealing. Match Performance, at 71 to 75, looks fully priced.

The various corners markets look more interesting. Cross-corners, priced at 24 to 27, looks cheap. This is a made-up market. It multiplies Man U's final corner count by Newcastle's. Both of these teams, as you would expect, win a lot of corners. Soccerbase reports that Man U get 6 on average, Newcastle 6.6. Multiply those together and you get 39.6. Furthermore, Man U get 7.5 on average at home, while Newcastle get an average of 5 per game on the road. Multiply those together and you get a make-up of 37.5. Both prices are well above the buy price. Neither gives away many corners (3.6 and 4.6, respectively), which explains the low price, but in this case you are betting on the two attacks, not their defences. You buy Cross-corners at 27 at £5.

The game begins as a lively affair. Both teams attack aggressively. Within twenty minutes there have been 5 corners, split 2–3, and the bet is looking good. Man U go ahead 1–0 on a goal by Van Nistelrooy, but Newcastle hold them there till half-time. By the break, there have been four corners each. So Cross-corners are already at 16. You need three more in the second half to put you into profit. Five corners to one team and six to the other would make Cross-corners up to 30.

This market is not offered in the running: you can only buy and sell before kick-off, or during the half-time break. The bookies now offer it at 47 to sell, 50 to buy. This is tempting: the corners were slowing down in the first half as both sides tired. As you bought at 27, you can collect a juicy £100 profit by selling at 47. But with the score tight, it looks like the attacking play will continue. You decide to stand pat.

Five minutes into the second half Scholes scores a quick goal to make it 2–0 and suddenly all the air goes out of the game. Newcastle are not going to come back from two goals down at Old Trafford and the game ends up in the midfield. There are no more flag kicks until well past the 60th minute, and just three more in total. The make-up is 30 – with 6 corners for Man U and 5 for Newcastle. As you bought at 27 at £5 a point, you make a measly £15. If you had sold at half-time it would have been £100.

Multiplying together the two teams' corners is a complicated basis for a bet, but it has some justification for intelligent gamblers. If the two attacks are evenly matched, this will push the total higher, whereas a heavy imbalance to one side will keep it down. In a game with ten corners, if they are split evenly, five apiece, the Cross-corners will make up at 25. But if one side gets eight and the other only two, it will settle at 16. If one side gets all ten corners, the market will make up at zero.

This is not how most punters approach the market, which suggests there is value for those who use their heads. Even more popular than Cross-corners is the market for Multi-corners. Here the bookies multiply all the first-half corners won by both teams by all those in the second half. It is even less predictable. A lot of gamblers love it.

It is a cold, rainy, gale-swept winter day and Middlesbrough are at home to Charlton. Boro are struggling near the relegation zone and need a victory, but both teams are defensively strong. There is little to choose between the sides. Add in the cold and the rain and the odds favour a dull game at the Riverside Stadium with few chances.

There may be value in betting on a low number of corners in the match. These two teams give up few apiece. Boro concede on average just 3.4 per game, thanks to a solid defence that includes Gareth Southgate. Charlton concede more, but still fewer than six per game. Add their averages together and you would expect nine corners a game. The price for total corners is 10 to 11. This is an unattractive sell. However, Multi-corners looks a better bet. The price before kick-off is 28 to sell. If Boro get three corners and Charlton six, as their form this season would suggest, that would produce nine corners in the match. If, as a worst-case scenario, they are split five and four between the halves, this would still make-up at 20. I sell at 28 at £10 a point.

There is nothing like an unpleasant, ground-out loss to make you remember every detail, even of something you would like to forget – like a dull, cold, wet league game between Middlesbrough and Charlton. There was nothing wrong with the strategy. There was little play down the wings, the ball spent most of the time in or around midfield. Attack was weak, there were few chances, and long balls down the flanks were run out by defenders, not turned in by forwards.

But both defences were having bad nights. This did not produce lots of goals, which would have made the game interesting. It merely produced lots of corners. For anyone short of corners, everything went wrong. A free-kick just before half-time forced Charlton's Dean Kiely to make a spectacular over-the-bar save: add on another one to make the interval corner count seven. The bookies moved the price to 38 to 42, predicting another six in the second half. This was too high to buy back, but too low to double up comfortably by selling more. I stood pat.

The first ten minutes of the second half went well. Then Boro won a dubious corner that had me yelling at the television set, and they started coming again. In the 70th minute any hope of profit evaporated when Mark Crossley had to tip over a sharp strike from Charlton's Chris Bart-Williams. This was the fourth corner of the second half. Multiply that by the seven won before the break and the Multi-corners already totalled 28 – with twenty minutes to go.

Here is where your losses can start soaring. Multi-corners is a highly leveraged market – which means a small number of events on the pitch can have a big effect on your bank account. Thanks to the seven in the first half, each corner now will add seven to the Multi-corners total. As I sold at £10 a point, each one will cost me £70. Ouch.

Moments later a blunder in the Charlton defence adds another. With gritted teeth I hear the commentator say, '. . . and Charlton really just gifted Middlesbrough a free corner there'. I am clutching my head and groaning. Multi-corners now stands at 35, I am already down £70, and there is another quarter of an hour to go. Each second grinds away.

Every time Charlton attack down the wing, I fear the worst, but the players turn back and play to the middle. I can barely look by the time the final whistle goes. Multi-corners made up at 35; I lost £70. Two more corners and that would have been £210. All things considered, I was lucky.

Selling Multi-corners is a dangerous game. For that reason some regular gamblers love it. The fear of those horrendous, escalating losses deters amateurs. Professionals reason, therefore, that the price is always set a little too high. Veteran punter John Hall says, 'I made quite a lot of money selling Multi-corners over the past three or four years. The price was usually around 34 to 35. But they've got wise to this and the prices have been dropped down to around 24 to 27. I still sell sometimes. I wouldn't in lower-division games or in Scottish games, where you can have a lot of corners. But I might still sell, for example, when it's Newcastle versus Arsenal.'

Jocky, a good friend in the City, loves to bet on Multis and it is his most profitable market. He says, 'I usually like to sell Multis, because I think they still tend to be priced too high. If a team doesn't have any width, or if they like to build it up slowly from the back, then they're not going to get a lot of corners. I think the Spanish league sees lower counts for that reason. But, for example, when Chelsea play Zenden – he crosses the ball in a lot – you see a lot of corners.' He did well going short of Liverpool Multis through the 2001/2 season. Later he recalled, 'Do you realise when Liverpool beat Ipswich five–nil on the last day, they didn't win a single corner? Not one. Ipswich won the match seven–nil – on corners.'

I prefer playing corners in running, which limits me to the Total Corners market. The spread, at 10 per cent of the average make-up, allows in-and-out trading. The absence of the multiplier effect means you know how much you are in for. An attacking game may or may not produce lots of goals, but if it features play down the wings it will almost certainly produce plenty of corners.

It is in corners that the growing influence of spread betting can most easily be seen. It is largely to satisfy the army of betters that TV companies such as Sky will flash up on the screen the number of corners each side has won so far. Those unaware of the market must wonder why they are being given this information. But there are plenty of people out there watching the game who care much more about who is leading on corners than who has scored more goals.

6

Half-time

The teams have gone back to their dressing-rooms to nurse their wounds and recover from the first forty-five minutes. The team trailing at the break is getting a roasting from the manager. The leaders are being urged to keep it up for the second half. On the field, ball boys and substitutes are kicking balls around. Behind the stands there are long queues for coffee and the loos. The coffee-shop staff, surprised as always when so many football fans appear at once, have made no preparations and there will be a long wait while they search for cups. There seems to be nothing to do for fifteen minutes. Time for a little history.

Spread betting began in 1974, when a young, unemployed stockbroker launched the first specialist firm. Stuart Wheeler had been fired by one merchant bank 'for managing their investments so badly', as he puts it, and by another because there was no work around. It was a terrible time in the City. The secondary banking crisis, the worst stock market slump since the war, crippling tax rates, the oil crisis, soaring inflation and the approach of the public finance crisis that would bring in the IMF in 1976 had together sounded the death knell of the go-go years of the early 1970s. 'There was nothing for me to do,' says Wheeler.

The only action in town was in gold. America was about to lift its restrictions on purchases by the public, and the price was rising as markets predicted a huge surge in sales. But in Britain it was virtually impossible for people to speculate on the metal. Gold was traded in US dollars, and the government levied hefty taxes on the foreign currency purchases needed to buy gold. Wheeler realised that people did not need to purchase gold physically to speculate on the price – they could simply place bets. No metal, or for that matter dollars, needed to change hands.

Someone had had this idea previously. Coral, the book-maker, already operated a business called Coral Index that allowed speculation in commodities along these lines. But it was a small operation, neglected by the fixed odds book-makers. Wheeler tried to interest Ladbrokes and William Hill in launching a rival, but neither was interested. They would later come to rue their mistake. Without a job or funds, Wheeler decided to raise money and do it himself.

He needed two things: backers and the help of a big gold-trading firm that would allow him to lay off some of the bets. With the help of a longstanding friend, Tommy Richter, he raised £100,000 – a vast sum at the time, especially given the financial collapse going on around him. Finding a friend among the gold traders seemed an even taller task.

The benchmark world gold price is set, twice a day, in the offices of N.M. Rothschild, the merchant bank, in St James's, London. Those involved in setting the price constitute a closed elite. Just five firms participate in the gold 'Fix'. At the time their power and prestige were huge. Gold had underpinned the global financial system since the Second World War. The surge in price and interest during the 1970s, as roaring inflation devalued every paper currency, made them more powerful than ever. With little hope, Wheeler tactfully made approaches. One of the firms, Mocatta & Goldsmid, agreed to help out. To this day, their decision seems incomprehensible, if fortunate. 'Why they agreed to do that with a tiny bookmaker like us I shall never know,' says Wheeler, 'but I am eternally grateful.' He was under way. The new firm would be called Investors' Gold Index, later shortened to IG.

It was only when he was putting the finishing touches to the plan and preparing to launch the company that Wheeler discovered a facet to spread betting that was to prove critical to its success. It is, essentially, tax free. Trades made with a spread betting firm count as bets, not investments, so winnings were subject only to a small betting tax and not to capital gains. In the 1970s, when capital gains tax peaked above 90 per cent, this gave the spread firms a compelling advantage. It was, in effect, a government subsidy to the new industry.

IG opened its doors in May 1975, anticipating the boom in gold to continue. The price responded by slumping. US demand proved to be much smaller than expected and in any case bubbles always burst. But the firm's tax advantage allowed it to move swiftly into other markets. It offered clients the chance to bet on the prices of other metals such as copper, lead and zinc, and so-called 'soft' commodities such as sugar, coffee and cocoa.

The overheads were low. IG began operations from Tommy Richter's offices in St James's Place. Soon it moved to the Wheelers' home in Chelsea. When the Wheelers' first child was born the family moved to Clapham – and so did the business. 'Everyone would come downstairs and have lunch with my one-year-old baby,' Wheeler recalls. Business grew steadily until the end of the decade. Then, over the course of three years, its fortunes were transformed by outside events.

The Russian invasion of Afghanistan, the fall of the Shah of Iran and runaway inflation sparked a second, and far bigger, gold bubble in 1979. The metal's price rocketed, peaking at nearly $1,000 an ounce in early 1980. It was a classic mania. Ordinary people lined up in the winter cold outside gold dealers' offices in Hatton Gardens, central London, clutching gold jewellery, candlesticks, picture frames and heirlooms to sell.

Around the same time the new Thatcher government began liberalising trade and freeing up exchange controls. IG responded swiftly and began offering markets on foreign currencies as well as commodities. The boom years of the 1980s had begun.

The most important change of all came in 1982, when bright sparks in the financial markets began offering contracts on Wall Street's Dow Jones Industrial Average and London's *Financial Times* All Share Index. For the first time, investors could bet on the movements of the entire stock market, by buying the relevant contract, rather than just on individual shares. Wheeler quickly launched spread bets on the same contracts. It brought out ordinary punters for the first time. He says, 'People may not have a view about the price of copper or sugar, but most had an idea of where they thought the stock market was going.'

Business took off. 'We were making fifty, maybe sixty thousand pounds a year. Within six months the stock index contracts were half our business,' says Wheeler. IG grabbed business thanks to two advantages over regular City trading. The first was the tax advantage. The second was that the betting was highly geared, which meant you could make big gains, or equally big losses, with only a small stake. For most people, buying a contract involved a significant outlay, and yielded relatively small gains. Taking a bet offered more action – and more risk – for much smaller investment.

The most interest came from private investors, jumping back into the stock market for the first time since the early 1970s, and in record numbers. 'It was a retail business,' says Wheeler. 'It was completely amazing that people would do business with us, a small company they hardly knew anything about.' IG placed a small advert in the *Financial Times* and money poured in. 'Someone sent in a ten thousand-pound cheque, knowing nothing about us at all. It was a moment of transformation for the business.'

IG's success had not gone unnoticed. In 1976, just one year after Wheeler began operations, Ladbrokes had had second thoughts and decided to launch a rival. The famous bookmaker's colourful boss, Cyril Stein, looked for a Young Turk to head the new operation. He soon alighted on the talented City trader and analyst Jonathan Sparke, then working for the industrial holding company Grovewood Securities. It was to prove an inspired choice for the industry, although not for Ladbrokes.

Ladbrokes and Sparke began delicate negotiations. Sparke wanted 25 per cent of the equity in the new venture, and a guarantee of one year's salary. If the new business became a success, both he and Ladbrokes would profit enormously. But his hand was weakened when Grovewood learned of the negotiations and fired him.

Sparke blamed Ladbrokes for the leak and refused to join the firm. Instead he found another job in the City, but his interest in spread betting had been awakened. Three years later, in early 1979, he made the jump and joined Coral Index. An old friend, Chris Hales, was running the operation. For the next two years the pair worked together, gaining invaluable experience in the running of a spread betting operation. They might have stayed much longer, locked away in a small operation inside the bookmaker, but then, through bizarre happenstance, Cyril Stein raised his head once more.

Coral was left vulnerable after a messy tit-for-tat with Ladbrokes led to a run-in with the gaming authorities, and Bass, the brewer, took it over. Bass wanted to sell its beer in Pontin's holiday camps, which Coral then owned, but wanted nothing to do with the small spread betting operation, which was both incomprehensible and risky. So Bass sold Coral Index to Ladbrokes. Sparke and Stein met again: '"Ah, you," Cyril Stein said to me when I walked in the door,' Sparke recalls.

Coral and Ladbrokes Indexes were merged and for a second time Sparke tried negotiating with Stein, with equal frustration. Talks over equity stakes dragged on while the business grew, until Stein announced that the price had gone up. So Hales and Sparke quit to launch their own business. They persuaded US company RevCo to back them, investing $3 million for 50 per cent of the equity. Their new firm, City Index, would take the industry a step beyond IG and launch spread betting on sports.

Stein called in his lawyers, but Sparke and Hales came out the better from the settlement talks, even clutching a copy of the Ladbrokes Index client list. 'They had made us agree that we would not try to poach their clients,' says Sparke, laughing. 'They thought they were being clever. But when the documents were signed we demanded the list. We said we needed it to know who we couldn't poach.'

In early 1983 the new firm placed an advertisement in the *Financial Times*, on the back page just below the Lex column. It resembled a party invitation, and read: 'Chris

Hales and Jonathan Sparke invite you to play the markets.
RSVP . . .'

They were stunned by the response. Money poured in,
just as it did for Wheeler at IG. The new firm began trading
the *FT* All Share and the Dow, and soon moved into other
markets, such as T-bills, commodities and currencies.
Clients wanted more. 'They started calling up and saying,
"My horse is racing at Cheltenham tomorrow. Is there any
way you can offer me a price?"'

No one had ever tried spread betting on sports. There
was no underlying commodity or index, as there was for
gold or the Dow, to trade off. But Sparke started thinking
about a riotous evening in Paris three years before, in
1979. He was there with Chris Hales and a friend, Michael
Spencer, then a young stockbroker and later the founder
of the moneybroker ICAP. They were in Paris for the
horseracing at Longchamps, the grand course west of the
City in the Bois de Boulogne. 'It was the year Three
Troikas won the Arc de Triomphe,' says Sparke. 'It had
been one of those crazy days. Longchamps was teeming.
We all drank far too much. At one point we sat under a
horse-chestnut tree and bet on who would get hit next by
a falling conker.'

Spencer won a bundle with a bet on Three Troikas, and
that evening the trio headed into Paris. By the small hours
of the morning they were sitting in a restaurant on the
Left Bank. 'All the big restaurants were either closed for
the weekend or booked up,' says Sparke. 'We were betting
on everything that day. When the waiter arrived with the
coffees someone – I think it was Michael – grabbed the
sugar bowl, turned it upside down and said, "OK, how
many lumps are in the bowl? You can buy at nine, or sell
at eight."' He was applying spread betting, rather than
fixed odds, to a non-financial bet. Sparke continues, 'We

started betting, and pretty soon we were trading our positions back and forth between us. I don't remember how many lumps there were in the end. We had all had far too much to drink.'

Sparke remembered that evening as he pondered the idea of spread betting on sports. If you could make a 'market' for fun on sugar lumps, why not on anything else? It was a simple step for City Index to begin offering prices on horses' winning distances, so that you could, for example, buy the favourite to win by more or less than three lengths. If you bought, and it romped home by ten lengths, you would be in clover. If you bought and it finished last, heaven help you.

City Index launched sports spread betting in 1984 on an ad hoc basis. Clients loved it. Sparke became more interested. He began working out how to apply spreads more generally to non-financials. Wimbledon was coming up. He sat down to devise a way of creating prices for the entire tournament: 'I wanted to create a system where you didn't have to pick the winner. You could simply bet that someone would do better than expected.' Something of this kind was needed to keep gamblers interested as John McEnroe, then playing the best tennis of his career, was a shoo-in for the title that year. Sparke's revolutionary invention was the 100 Index, where you get 100 points if your player wins, 70 if he comes second, and so on down to a handful of points for each player who makes it to the last sixteen. He says, 'It introduced a new concept. It wasn't just about who wins. If you find a no-hoper who goes a long way, you can make many times your money. We then started applying it to football, in 1985. That's when things really started to hum.'

Despite the growing popularity of sports betting, by far the bulk of the business was still in financials.

Privatisations and the bull market of the 1980s generated huge interest in the stock market, and, among other things, powered spread betting on to greater and greater success. Business boomed through the middle of the decade. By the summer of 1987 City and IG were coining it. In the twelve months to May 1987, IG made £700,000 pretax profits. During the following four months it made another £700,000. Wheeler recalls, 'It was obvious we were going to make one or even two million, and we planned to float on the stock market the following summer.'

But the success story was to be rudely interrupted. On Monday, 19 October 1987 stock markets around the world crashed. Billions of pounds of paper wealth were destroyed. Private punters who traded on credit, the prime recruiting ground for the spread firms, were wiped out. Confidence in the markets evaporated overnight. And the spread firms nearly disappeared too. They were heavily exposed to the collapse, and the clientele vanished.

City Index had to borrow $11.5 million overnight just to stay afloat, paying 21 per cent interest on the bailout. Wheeler's IG fared little better: 'It was an absolutely appalling, harrowing week,' he recalls. It would be thirteen years before his company was finally floated.

Stock markets boom and stock markets bust, but football carries on. Financial betting slumped after the crash, but the spread betting on sports continued to grow. In Edinburgh two university students began offering spreads on major sporting events, operating a small business by phone from their digs in the doubtless long, empty hours between essays. Meanwhile, on the floor of the stock exchange a young broker, disillusioned with the market in the aftermath of the crash and finding time on his hands, began creating markets in an amateur, ad hoc way. He found a lot of business among the other brokers, who also now had lots of free time on their hands. When he and the Edinburgh students collided sports betting suddenly took off.

In the spring of 1991 Compton Hellyer, then a derivatives analyst in the City and a keen gambler, took a call from his landlady Woody Clark. The pair owned a racehorse together. She had a business proposition to put to him. She had just had lunch with Angus Hamilton, one of the two Edinburgh students who ran Spread Bet International. Unlike City and IG, it made markets only on sporting events, and business was booming. He and his business partner, fellow-student Paul Johnson, were looking for outside investors. The business was growing too fast for them to handle on their own. Was Hellyer interested? He was, and met the pair in London. 'They were little boys, still at university,' he says. But he loved the idea, which he grasped immediately: 'It was the only time anyone came to me with an idea I could understand.' He offered to help raise the money, taking over as chairman and taking an equity stake.

They set out to raise £250,000. One of the companies Hellyer approached was IG Index. But Wheeler, in a foolish move echoing Ladbrokes' short-sightedness fifteen years before, turned them down. He could see no great future in spread betting on sports. Others were more forthcoming, and the trio raised £400,000.

They began preparations to launch the firm professionally in the new year, 1992, as Sporting Index. Whereas IG had effectively launched spread betting as a serious business, and City Index first applied the principles to events outside the financial markets, Sporting Index would take the sports market to a new level.

Complicating matters, though, a court ruling at that time concluded that spread bets were contracts, rather than gambling debts, and so were legally enforceable. (Under English law gambling debts are considered 'debts of honour' and cannot be enforced in law.) The change meant that the spread firms, including Sporting, could collect debts more easily, but it also meant they had to be regulated and comply with sometimes onerous rules. This required extra work and delayed the firm's launch. Sporting Index finally opened 'on April Fool's Day in 1992', says Hellyer. 'The only thing going on was the general election.' So their first 'sports' market was on that.

Meanwhile, Wheeler had performed an about-face every bit as quick as Cyril Stein's. IG Index launched its first spread bets on sports and also made a market on the election. Whereas a year before City Index had had sports spread betting largely to itself, there were now three firms in hot competition.

Interest in the election was high. Following the two Conservative landslides of the previous decade 1992 offered a sporting race. It was the closest election of modern times. Right until election day the opinion polls confidently predicted a Labour victory. The BBC, indeed, was still predicting one for several hours after the polls closed. But a sharp move against Labour began a week before polling, helped by an over-the-top Labour rally at which the party leader, Neil Kinnock, arrived by helicopter. Wags quickly dubbed it the 'Nuremberg Rally'. The triumphalist meeting fed long-term, nagging doubts among many voters about Kinnock's suitability for the job of prime minister.

The shift did not show up in the polls, but they were evident at IG Index. Wheeler recalls, 'From the Sunday we suddenly saw the smart money coming in on the Tories in a big way.' Sporting was not as lucky as IG. Its prices reflected the polls and the team were dumbfounded by the

Tories' surprise victory. It lost money, but, says Hellyer, 'we only had fifteen clients, so it didn't matter'.

Nevertheless, the business was up and running. It turned its attention to horseracing, offering prices for a few dedicated customers. Initially, the handful of staff who constituted Sporting Index met once a week. 'We sat in my little office in South Kensington,' says Hellyer. 'If someone had bet fifty pounds on the horses we sat there watching TV to see the result.' But business grew rapidly: 'Within three months we found ourselves working full time for the company. It just took off.'

Much of Sporting's success was due to one of its first recruits, and certainly its most important. David Garbacz was an options trader who became bored and disillusioned with the City following the 1987 crash. He was one of Spread Bet International's first clients, and kept himself occupied during the day making markets in sports events. 'I spent five per cent of my time selling options, and ninety-five per cent making markets in other things – football, Wimbledon, and so on,' he recalls. After a disastrous Wimbledon, he had a queue of 150 people demanding money: 'They wouldn't take a cheque either,' he moans.

When the new firm offered him a job he jumped at the chance. Most of the markets that exist today he helped launch. 'The markets at the time were very limited,' he remembers. 'On football it was just Supremacy and Total Goals. There was no innovation. It was my aim to take things and make them more active. We introduced shirt numbers, corners, things like that. I started these up early on. People asked, "How can you bet on the number of corners in a game?"'

They quickly worked it out. Hellyer says, 'We started it at the same time as satellite TV. We live off TV. If

Manchester United are playing Arsenal and it's not on TV, and Walsall are playing Coventry and it is televised, most of our bets will be on the Walsall game.' The business quickly needed new funds to handle the growth. Within its first year it had to raise another £700,000. In 1994 Sporting needed another £2 million. Hellyer raised this in one evening over a bottle of champagne with Michael Stoddart, the chairman of City fund manager Electra. 'He called me at nine the next morning and said, "I read your proposal in bed last night. We've decided to do it."'

The firms have had more than their share of disasters and blunders along the way. Brian Lara nearly put Sporting out of business early in its career when the young West Indian batsman scored his record 375 runs in the Antigua Test. Clients were heavily long of West Indian runs, leaving the bookmakers by default betting on a low number. 'It was horrendous,' says Hellyer. 'He was in for three days. Every time he hit a four it cost us fifteen hundred pounds. We were sitting there bleeding to death.' Add together the bets on Lara's Runs for the Innings, West Indies' Runs for the Match, and Runs for the Series and Lara's stand cost Sporting alone nearly £100,000, and other firms similar sums. But it was to prove a marketing coup for the industry. The newspapers were full of stories of big winnings and it introduced the concept of spread betting to the public.

Tony Holden, royal biographer and Gooner, although not necessarily in that order, made £2,750 from Lara's innings, buying at £10 early on at 80. He later told John Edwards, my colleague at the *Mail*, 'The guy was still making me money when I went to sleep on two nights. And all day. You know, I was stuck in a taxi at some broken traffic lights listening on a transistor and the driver apologised for the delay. I said not to worry because Lara had made me ninety pounds since we pulled up.' Holden was doubly lucky. He did not realise at the time that he could sell the bet back for a profit in the running. So he let it run and run . . . all the way to the boundary, as it were.

Simon Cawkwell, an infamous City bear-raider who made his name going short of shares in Robert Maxwell's MGN empire, took an opposing view. 'I was watching it on television and I felt sure the West Indies were about to collapse. I sold their Total Innings Runs rather heavily just as that chap Lara was walking out to the crease.' He lost £30,000.

Then there was the 1995 Rugby World Cup game between New Zealand and Japan, another early disaster for the industry. When the All Blacks, the overwhelming favourites, announced they would only field their reserves, the bookmakers slashed their prices, predicting the All Blacks would score only around 72 points, winning by around 40.

Ian Robertson, the sports broadcaster, was in South Africa for the tournament. When he heard the price, he rushed to a telephone and bought New Zealand. As he later explained to Compton Hellyer at Sporting, he knew that every member of the New Zealand team would be playing for his life, hoping to make it into the first fifteen. He cleaned up, collecting a huge profit as the All Blacks romped home 145 to 17. 'He still dines out on the story,' says Hellyer, ruefully. City Index later disclosed it lost £120,000 overall on the game, or £25 a second.

The firms also grossly underestimated the number of bookings during the Euro 96 football championships. 'We made a complete Horlicks,' says Hellyer. 'The referees were told to get tough, and we got taken out by a number of professional punters.'

The blunders in the early years were not confined to

prices. During an Australian Open tennis tournament in the mid-1990s, Sporting accidentally made a market on a match that had already ended. 'The results were in that morning's *Daily Telegraph* when we put up our prices,' says Hellyer. 'We took forty bets on the match. Amazingly, twenty of those were losing bets.' The company paid out on the winning bets, and cancelled the losing ones, putting the whole exercise down to marketing – and experience.

The spread firms survived these blunders because punters, at the time, were unsophisticated. There was so little data available that very few people knew what the correct prices should have been. 'You look back with amazement at some of the prices we were setting,' says a senior market-maker at Sporting. 'We were offering Corners at 13 to 14 for an FA Cup Final, and Shirt Numbers at 26 to 29 in the days when the players were wearing 1 through 11' (see Chapter 7 for details of Shirt Number betting). Still punters bought at what were absurdly high levels.

More serious have been the outbreaks of market rigging involving players. Spread betting, with its wide variety of markets, is especially open to abuse because so many of its markets are not material to the outcome.

Rigging first emerged in horseracing. City Index offered a price on the aggregate winning distances of the successful horses in six races. Jockeys are required to do their best to win a race and deliberately losing is a serious offence. But there is no rule saying they have to win by the biggest margin they can. So City Index noticed certain clients would sell total winning distances for minor meets where several odds-on favourites were running. The jockeys then obliged to keep the lengths down. Sparke says: 'They would come to the last hurdle leading by ten lengths. Then they would pull up, and pull up, and pull up, and win by a length. We'd even see them on their mobiles afterwards, talking about it. At one meet we lost twenty-five thousand.' There was no question about what was going on. In most cases those placing bets were connected with the stable. In some instances they owned the horses. Sparke recalls: 'One admitted it to me outright. He asked: "Tell me what I'm doing wrong." I said: "All right, but from now on I'm limiting you to £10 a length." Jockeys aren't allowed to gamble, but there are plenty of ways around that.'

Rigging also hit cricket. City for a while offered a price on when the first no ball would be delivered in a match. Sparke remembers in one 1990s Test match a relative of an opening bowler heavily sold the time of the first no ball: 'The bowler was so desperate to deliver a no ball on his first delivery that his foot landed a good twelve inches beyond the line. But the umpire didn't call it. On his second delivery his foot was practically halfway down the pitch.'

In football the problem arose after Sporting launched what was soon to become its most controversial market, the Time of First Throw-in. The market's volatility had become apparent soon after it was launched, during Euro 96. The Time for the First Throw-in was priced around 90 seconds, and punters made small profits selling it for the first handful of games. 'Then came, I think, Scotland against Holland,' says one market-maker at Sporting. 'The ball didn't go out of play for ten minutes. You had guys who sold at a tenner a second, who lost six hundred pounds. We made fifty thousand pounds in the first ten minutes of the match.'

This volatility quickly caught the eye of those directly involved in football. The market was so frivolous, and so immaterial to the final outcome of the game, that it was asking for abuse. It got it. For one game, recalls David Garbacz, who invented the market while at Sporting Index, 'we had priced the market quite high, at 100 seconds. Just before kick-off we saw a steady stream of sellers. We dropped the price quickly. By the kick-off it was down to 40 to 50 seconds. As soon as the whistle went, a player kicked the ball straight out.'

The financial regulators intervened and Sporting scrapped the market. Garbacz still regrets that. 'It was very, very popular. It gave you that early fix,' he says. 'All the other companies copied it. I remember one game, I think it was Liverpool against Paris St Germain, where the ball didn't go out for fourteen minutes. I was upset when it was abandoned.'

Controversy is not confined to sports spread betting. The financials business, which remains much bigger than sports, was brought to the public eye last year by two incidents.

In the first affair the police launched an investigation into spread betting on shares by five young stockbrokers. Fraud detectives alleged the group had collected £2.2 million in profit by dealing on inside information, using spread firms instead of the stock market in the hope of avoiding detection. The facts of the case remain unknown at the time of writing, so there is no reason to assume the trio were guilty of anything. However, the incident highlighted the vulnerability of the spread firms. Those who are seeking to trade on inside information might be tempted to bet on the shares at IG or City Index, instead of buying shares directly on the stock market, on the assumption that the trades are less closely scrutinised by the regulators. This is not the case. The spread firms report every trade to the Financial Services Authority. Spread volumes are tiny compared to those on the stock exchange, so a suspicious trade is much more likely to stand out. However, the bandits will continue to try.

The closeness of the regulation came home to me when a City friend thought the overall stock market was likely to go down. She placed an innocent bet to that effect with a spread firm, where she has an account she usually uses for sports betting. 'I got a call the next morning from our compliance department, screaming at me. The FSA had called them up and reported the trade,' she says. She does not even work on the shares side at her investment bank, so there was no suggestion of a conflict of interest. Her compliance department was upset that she had bet on the market falling. The City still lives off the mantra that the market always rises. Staff turning pessimistic could be bad for business.

Another colourful incident which put spread betting in the public eye arose in early 2002. The entrepreneur Paul Davidson, known in the City as 'The Plumber', was a major shareholder in a tiny company called Cyprotex that was due to float on the stock market. Apparently convinced the shares would rise, he placed a £6 million bet to that effect with City Index by buying the shares on the spreads. What followed was farcical. City needed to lay off the bet, and did so in a transaction with the investment bank Dresdner Kleinwort Wasserstein. Dresdner in turn needed to lay its bet, and did so by buying shares when the company floated. To cover the risk, it had to buy nearly all the Cyprotex shares for sale. The net result was that the Cyprotex flotation went very well indeed, huge demand coming from . . . Dresdner Kleinwort Wasserstein. Some cried foul, but the Plumber pleaded innocence. He said he did not realise how City Index would hedge its position. He lost money on the bet in the aftermath. You would hardly risk £6 million in this way if you knew what you were doing. But being known as the Plumber did not help his case in the papers.

News of the curious deal was broken on the front page of the *Financial Times* and sent waves through the industry. A senior figure at one firm quickly called Compton Hellyer at Sporting to discuss what they should do. Hellyer was the chairman of the industry body, the Spread Betting Association. However, he had not seen the story. 'I don't read the *Financial Times*,' he explained. 'I only read the *Racing Post*.'

The spreads industry ballooned in the late 1990s, driven by the boom on the stock market that, first, put money in the pockets of spread-savvy City dealers and, second, attracted more and more ordinary people into the market. Peter Harris, one of the founders of Sporting Index, left and launched his own firm, Spreadex. In early 2000 US broker Cantor Fitzgerald, attracted by the boom in online share dealing, launched a fourth operation, Cantor Index.

Financial spread betting remains by far the biggest part of the business. It is dominated by IG. 'I'd far rather be a shareholder in IG than Sporting Index,' admits Compton Hellyer, Sporting's chairman, 'but it's more fun working here.' The industry marked an interesting and tragic milestone on 11 September 2001. I was, by chance, lunching with IG Index when a colleague of mine from the *Mail* came up and told us a plane had flown into one of the Twin Towers in New York. This came a week after a small private plane had flown into the Statue of Liberty and we assumed – like everyone else, apparently – that this was a similar incident. As we were leaving shortly afterwards my companion's mobile began to ring. He took the call and the scale of what had happened became clear. IG made the decision to continue to make a price on New York's main stock market indicator, the Dow Jones Industrial

Average. Others followed suit. Wall Street was to remain closed for a week, as was the Chicago derivatives market. During that time the spread firms were the only places in the world where you could trade the US market. It was a gruesome coming of age.

By pure coincidence, 11 September touched the spread firms directly in other ways. Cantor Index is part of the US stockbroking firm Cantor Fitzgerald, which lost 658 staff that day. It occupied the floors nearest to where the first plane hit. Horror stories came out from the firm on both sides of the Atlantic – the planes hit during a conference call between the two offices – and Cantor Index staff would be visibly shaken by any reference to the massacre over six months later. By another coincidence, Michael Spencer's firm ICAP also occupied one of the towers. Hundreds of staff worked there. Extraordinarily, all but one escaped before the building came down. Nevertheless, it would be camped out in loaned accommodation for months before opening new offices of its own. Three months later ICAP held its charity day, an annual event when all the proceeds from the day's work are given to good causes. In 2001 a hefty slice went to support victims of the terrorist attack.

The financials' dominance of the spread betting industry is likely to change. It is already suffering a slow-down due to the stock market slump. When the markets recover, if spread betting continues to grow at the pace of the last twenty years the authorities are likely to intervene eventually and tax profits on financial bets as capital gains. Without that the spread firms will continue to take business away from the stock market, especially in the trading of small companies and penny shares. The stock market helps such companies raise money to grow and expand. Indeed, that is its purpose. Spread firms do not.

In contrast the sports side is only taking business away from the fixed odds rivals. Once you have started spread betting, you are unlikely to go back to the tortuous and limited options of fixed odds betting. I suspect the industry's future is more likely to lie on the sports side than on the financials'. The conventional wisdom in the City disagrees with me almost entirely, so I am probably right.

Cantor Index, the youngest spread firm, was launched in early 2000 to capitalise on the stock market boom that had sent dotcoms soaring. Lewis Findlay joined to head the operation in March of that year – the same month the dotcoms started collapsing. 'We had no intention of going into sports,' he admits. But as the market slump deepened they had second thoughts. Cantor hired David Garbacz from Sporting and launched its own sports operation in 2001.

Today sports spread betting has grown out of all recognition. It offers bets on sports as diverse as football, cricket, rugby union, rugby league, tennis, horseracing, greyhound racing, Formula One, US football, baseball and basketball. True to its roots, it also offers markets on politics.

The prices at the spread remain, as in 1992 at IG, a better predictor of general election outcomes than occasional opinion polls. People will tell pollsters anything.

They are called at home when they are putting the baby to bed, or accosted on the high street when they are rushing to catch the bus. They might be moved by momentary pique, boredom or impatience. When people risk their own money they take a more considered view. Furthermore a handful of politicians, and political journalists with access to the inside scoop, are active clients and some are not averse to dealing on inside information. This was demonstrated in the summer of 2000 when a petrol shortage quickly boiled over into a crisis as truck-drivers besieged refineries. With a general election due eight or nine months later, opinion polls suggested a dramatic swing in favour of the Conservatives. But at the spread firms the prediction for Labour's likely winning majority rose. The incident had revived the smart money's interest in the market, and it bet heavily on Labour. The spreads were proved right – or, rather, less wrong. They predicted a Labour majority of 100 seats. In the 2001 election Labour nearly repeated its unprecedented 1997 landslide, winning a majority of 167. My City trader pal Jocky, whose political antennae are almost never wrong, cleaned up. One of the spread firms even limited his stakes, complaining, 'This market is just supposed to be a bit of fun.'

There are other opportunities to make a profit. When the Conservatives held their leadership election in 2001, Michael Portillo was such a strong front runner that fixed odds firms refused to take bets. The spread firms offered a market on the likely percentage of the vote each candidate would receive in the final ballot. It was a three-stage election. First, sitting Conservative Members of Parliament voted. The weakest candidates were weeded out and then the MPs voted again. The two with the most votes then went before a ballot of all party members in the country. Jocky took a dim view of Portillo's chances and went short of his final ballot percentage at 50. He also went long of Iain Duncan-Smith, a strong outside candidate. He cleaned up as Portillo failed to make it to the final round, in which Duncan-Smith romped home.

The bookmakers also make markets on the Chancellor of the Exchequer's Budget speech every year, ranging from the number of times he will take a sip of water or mention certain buzz words to how much he will add to various tax rates.

I played poker with friends the night before the Budget. Jocky arrived clutching the prices list and what passes for form data – the make-ups from the previous year's Budget. We debated the merits of various prices. Three stood out as golden opportunities. The first related to the amount of tax likely to be put on each packet of cigarettes. The initial price was 20 to 22p, which looked way too high. Chancellor Gordon Brown, a preachy enemy of smoking, had raised the rate sharply in his early years in the job. The predictable result was that smuggling was soaring, and the Treasury's revenue from cigarette taxes had fallen. From the year before, he had contented himself with raising tax in line with inflation. This would suggest an increase of just 6p. Word of the bookie's price circulated around the City, where betting on the Budget speech is a major event. By the next morning the price slumped to 14 to sell. The Chancellor that afternoon raised the tax by 6p.

The second attractive market lay in the likely increase in the rate of the sales tax, VAT. It was then 17.5 per cent. The spread firms offered a market on what it would be after the Budget, setting an initial price of 18.2 to 18.4 per cent. This was also a clear sell. Although the New Labour government was itching to raise taxes to pay for a huge increase in health spending, VAT is far too much of a headline tax for them to touch. It is regressive, hitting the poorest hardest, and too symbolic. Gordon Brown likes raising taxes by stealth – a little here, a little there. It did not appear he wanted to be known as the man who put VAT up to 18.5 per cent. The government had been leaking plans to raise VAT in the papers the previous week. Anyone who knew the Blair government knew this was simply a softening-up exercise by New Labour, so that we would all feel pathetically grateful when they left VAT where it was. And so it proved.

The biggest opportunity lay in the markets for the number of times certain words would be mentioned. 'Health' and 'Education' were both priced at 7 to 9. The year before, health was mentioned just twice, education seven. Yet this was going to be the 'healthcare' Budget. The government had been badly spooked by growing anger over the crisis in the National Health Service. It planned to respond by throwing our money at the problem, in the hope that this would improve the opinion polls – excuse me, would improve the NHS. Everything was in place. A retired banker, Derek Wanless, would present his long-awaited report on rescuing the NHS on the morning of the Budget, and then Gordon Brown would stand up and raise taxes to pay for it.

In these circumstances a prediction of seven to nine mentions of 'health' was far too low. Education, on the other hand, was too high. Politicians are always told not to dilute their messages. If Brown wanted to sell huge tax rises to pay for the NHS, he would not then go on a long digression about the need for education. The smart move was to buy the former at 9, and sell the latter at 7 in the same quantity, betting simply that health would be mentioned much more often than education. Others spotted the same thing – but not until lunchtime on the day, when the price on health skyrocketed. It hit 14 to 16 shortly before the speech itself, allowing you to sell back for a juicy profit before the speech. The only danger, as one trader remarked to me, was that Brown would refer to New Labour's long-lost 1997 election pledge, to focus on 'education, education, education'. But it didn't happen. He mentioned health seventeen times, education six times.

The spread firms also make markets on overseas political events, such as the 2002 French presidential elections.

France was overcome by a wave of apathy, and in a low turnout National Front leader Jean-Marie Le Pen, who had once called the Nazi Holocaust a 'detail' of the Second World War, secured more votes than the Socialist Prime Minister Lionel Jospin to take second place and enter the second round of voting.

The spread firms predicted he would collect an extraordinary 23 to 25 per cent of the vote in the run-off against Jacques Chirac, the conservative incumbent. This was a clear sell: Le Pen had won just 16.8 per cent in the first round. It was reasonable to assume that anyone who wanted to vote for him and his fascist policies had done so then. So 17 per cent, give or take, was likely to be his limit. It was also reasonable to suppose that some people had voted for him in the first round simply out of protest against the mainstream parties, who were even more venal, arrogant and self-indulgent than is usually the case. They would be suitably embarrassed that he had come second and would vote for Chirac. And there would be many others who had not bothered voting first time around but would make sure they did in the second round. For once, every vote would count. The whole world would look at the final outcome to see just how many French people were nuts.

Selling at 22.5 per cent (the price had dropped quickly as others also took a bearish view) was profitable: Le Pen got 18.2 per cent.

Sporting Index today employs 180 people and dominates spread betting on sports. It has around 65 per cent of the market. IG has another 20 per cent, and the two newer firms, Cantor and Spreadex, share the rest. City Index lost its inspiration in the mid-1990s, when Jonathan Sparke retired. Michael Spencer, by then the majority owner, was more focused on building his ICAP brokerage business. It eventually quit the sports business altogether, selling its remaining sports book to Sporting. Ladbrokes, Corals and William Hill also backed out of the business. They had arrived too late. More importantly, the operations fitted poorly with their fixed odds businesses. Spread betting firms tend to employ livelier City traders who think quickly on their feet. Fixed odds firms set prices at head office, and give little or no leeway to the boys taking orders in the corner bookie shops. 'This is a totally different business,' says one market-maker, who worked for one of the fixed odds boys before making the jump to spreads. 'You need to do more than just write odds on a blackboard.'

Indeed you do. The trading rooms of the big spread betting firms are almost identical to those in the City, with traders sitting in front of computer screens taking phone calls. The action is fast. I visited IG on the night Liverpool hosted Roma, Man U played Boavista and Celtic played Motherwell. For those who weren't getting enough sporting action, dogs were also running at some strip-lit track or other. A bank of TV sets along one huge wall showed all of the events, and the bookies were making a market in each one.

A market? I lie. On Liverpool against Roma they were making five dozen markets, from Total Goals to bets on individual players' scoring chances. Overall that night they were offering, and updating, nearly 200 sets of prices.

Each game is the responsibility of a single market-maker, who is watching three computer screens. These show the firm's current prices and trading volumes, its net wins, losses and risks for every market, and live prices offered by rivals. They also have a live TV feed in one corner of one screen, showing the game. As if all this isn't enough, he has charts and tables in his hand to guide him as he updates prices during the game. Phone calls come through to traders, who shout out to him for updated prices. At certain moments the phones light up as the calls flood in. This happens just before kick-off, just after a goal or a booking and at half-time. As there are three football games going, the overall effect is chaotic.

'Second goal Liverpool, Chris.' 'Sixty-two, sixty-four.' 'Patrick, corners . . .' 'Nine and a half, ten and a half.' 'Last goal Man U?' 'Bookings Liverpool?' 'Bookings will be, uh, where are we, let's go thirty-four, thirty-eight.' 'Seventy, seventy-three the last goal.'

'Hang on, Montella and Delvecchio are on. Off the shirts!' 'Bookings, Gary!'

'You can have bookings at twenty-five, twenty-eight.' 'Total goals, Patrick!' 'Let's go two-point-three to two-point-five.'

'Go twenty, twenty-four.'

They continued in this vein for ninety minutes. Amazingly, no one seemed to answer out of turn or give the price for the wrong game. As far as I could tell.

Market-makers start setting prices days, weeks and sometimes months before the event. Whether they are covering Serie A or the Nationwide League, they will follow the market from the off season and try to keep track of every significant development, from transfers to injuries. 'As a specialist, it's your responsibility to know everything there is to know about the field you're covering,' says one. Pricing up a routine game can take a day's work.

The market-makers concede the growing complexity gives clever gamblers a potential edge. Lewis Findlay at Cantor Index, says, 'As a company, we make hundreds of prices. As a client, you can pick off just one.'

As with politics, mistakes are more likely when the market-makers are not specialists, and when the bookmakers are busy. You are more likely to find good opportunities the further you look away from the headline markets, such as Total Goals and Supremacy, and the big-name games. A senior market-maker at Sporting Index admits a few dedicated punters will beat him consistently by focusing on the Nationwide League. 'If I'm pricing up the games for the weekend, I have to rate seventy-two teams against each other in thirty-six games. If I get seventy-one teams correct, all they have to do is find the one where I'm wrong. They don't have to bet on the other games.'

Specialist punters have an additional advantage: the bookmakers have to work out prices with imperfect information. 'The punters have a real edge in the Nationwide League,' admits a market-maker at Sporting. 'Everyone knows what's going on in the Premiership, but not necessarily in the League. We can only go on the TV highlights and the reports we read.'

It is possible to beat the spreads on the big games, too. Those following a particular team will have an advantage over market-makers, who have to cover them all. Arsenal fans who were watching closely in 2001/2, for example, saw that Thierry Henry lost his goal-scoring edge into the last third of the season, while Robert Pires and Freddie Ljungberg were quietly stepping into the breach.

A small business has grown up of arbitrage specialists (known in the business as 'arbs') who try to exploit small pricing differences between the firms. If Spreadex lets you buy Bookings for a game at 35, and Sporting take a different view of the game and will let you sell at 38, it is possible to make a 3-point profit without any risk by buying with Spreadex and immediately selling at Sporting. No matter what happens, you make 3 points. You have effectively closed the trade. Of course, to do this you need to have lots of money and to move fast.

To make a decent profit you will need big credit limits or big balances with both firms. Although, in reality, as you don't know where the gap will arise, you will need it with *all four* of the big spread firms: IG, Sporting, Cantor and Spreadex. To make £300 from the trade, you will have to bet at £100 a point on both sides. To buy at Spreadex for that sum at 35 points you will need at least £3,500 on account there. Ditto at Sporting.

The *Racing Post* usually highlights any arbitrage possibilities in the morning. The spread firms open for business at 10 a.m. The arbs immediately pile in. The bookmakers view them with disdain. 'We've got a hard core who call up every Friday morning,' says Gary Hope at IG. 'We know who they are.' Increasingly the firms refuse to take the trade, especially when – as often happens – the arbs know so little about the game that they cannot even pronounce the names of the teams. 'We're not here for them,' says Gary. 'My favourite arb story was on the Chelsea–Gillingham game in last year's cup. There was an arbitrage on the Shirt Numbers. One punter bought them with one firm and sold with us. But he had a limited-risk, limited-profit account with the other company, so during the game his profits stopped with them while his losses carried on rising with us. He lost money. He ended up writing a letter to the *Racing Post*, complaining about bookmakers' inconsistency.'

The market-makers distinguish between the arbs who simply read prices in the *Racing Post* and 'technical arbs', people who make money by doing some work. Technical arbs work out ways to get an advantage by counterbalancing fixed odds bets and the spreads, or use prices on different markets to give themselves very favourable odds. 'If they've gone to the trouble to work it out, they'll make a bit of money off us and good luck to them,' says Paul Austin, marketing director at IG. He is not being disingenuous. Finding those opportunities is hard work. There are professionals who do it for a living, trading with the spreads and fixed odds firms in Britain, and with bookmakers in India and Southeast Asia, taking advantage of pricing differences. 'The introduction of spread betting has created an army of two to three hundred professional arbs,' says one market-marker. 'They make a living from arbitrage. They're dealing with bookmakers all around the world. It's not actually betting. It's risk free, or supposed to be. They bet as much money as they can.'

There remains one big difference between the sports and financial spread betting. On financials, prices reflect those in the 'real' international markets, and those are set by supply and demand. Brokers simply take their profits from the spread. If everyone is piling into gold, the price will rise. It doesn't matter if the market-maker thinks it is absurd and is bound to crash. He simply moves prices to match supply and demand. In sports this does not happen to the same extent. If the bookie thinks Bolton will beat Spurs, he will set prices to reflect this. If all the Spurs fans pile in betting the other way, he will move his prices slowly. The bookie takes a position. You are largely betting against the house.

In the early years of the industry this has worked for the bookies – on balance. 'We win fifty thousand a day for five days, and then on the sixth day we lose a hundred thousand,' says Sporting's Compton Hellyer. The bookmakers have traditionally been short of Goals, Bookings, Corners, Shirt Numbers, and big-name scorers such as Michael Owen. This means the punters have bought these markets, and there have been few, if any, sellers. So the house takes the downside position itself. When a match ends with no score and no bookings, the bookmakers collect huge winnings. Hellyer says, 'If a match ends four–three with three men sent off, that will cost us a hundred thousand. But we see it as money lent. We'll get it back.'

This is changing. Already the weight of money is starting to move prices significantly. You can see this in the final quarter of an hour before kick-off. It was also dramatically apparent in the weeks leading up to the 2002 World Cup. The prices for the most popular national teams, especially those of France and Italy, soared in the tournament markets as punters piled in. Those rose so far that anyone who bought them when the markets first opened could have sold long before the first ball was kicked for an easy profit. There is just too much business now. Flying casual is riskier, while the profits to be made from simply providing a market are rising.

The firms are also differently placed. IG Index has already floated on the stock market. Sporting now has an army of outside investors, and Hellyer expects the firm to float or be sold to a bigger company within the next few years. Outside investors do not want to be told your profits are up because you bet the house on Michael Owen missing a penalty and he hit the crossbar. Those are Nick Leeson profits. They lead, inevitably, to Nick Leeson results. Investors want to be told your profits are up because sales rose and you take a cut of every trade. Lewis Findlay explains: 'This business is all about getting to a critical mass, where you have enough two-way flow. The perfect world is where you have zero position going into every event, you're purely a broker. That would be perfect, but a little dull. The second-best situation would be where you only have the positions you choose. But there's a caveat: you need to choose right.'

In early 2002 a new spread-betting operation was launched to operate exactly like a financial market, moving prices solely in line with supply and demand. Trading Sports, unlike the traditional spread firms, said it would not take positions itself. Using technology derived from the insurance industry, it aimed just to match buyers and sellers. Ken Mulvany, the company's strategy director, said: 'We run a central exchange for the gambling industry. We pool the end users where they can transact with each other. We just provide the exchange, the way the New York Stock Exchange provides one for the likes of Merrill Lynch and Lehman.' A small operation out of Dublin, Intrade, already does something similar. Its main market, however, simply turns fixed odds bets into percentages. A team winning a game makes up at 100. If it is evens before the match, the price is 50, and so on. You can trade in and out.

These changes are excellent news for shrewd punters. You have a better chance of beating the public than you do of beating a market-maker who has done his research. The more prices are moved by the weight of money, the more opportunities will open up for someone who knows his football.

7

Shirt Numbers

Ade Akinbiyi is causing a rare case of nerves among the bookies. The striker has just signed on for Crystal Palace, and will get his first outing in tonight's match against Wolves. But the bookmakers aren't worrying about Akinbiyi. They are worried about what he is wearing.

Akinbiyi reportedly wanted shirt number 10 at his new club, but it was taken, so he chose the next-best thing – two 5s. With 55, his shirt carries one of the highest numbers in the league. This is proving a problem for the market-makers when they turn to the Shirt Numbers market. Shirt Numbers, which tallies not the number of goals in a match but the numbers worn by the scorers, is growing in popularity. That is largely because it carries high risk – and never more so than tonight. Wolves' chief scorers are Nathan Blake, wearing number 27, and Dean Sturridge, in number 29. Palace's are Clinton Morrison, wearing 10, and Dougie Freedman, in number 9. And then there is Akinbiyi.

A goalless draw will make up at zero. A 1–0 result is likely to make up anywhere between 9, if Freedman scores, and 55, if Akinbiyi does. Two goals could produce a result between 18 and 110, three between 27 and 165. A five-goal match, unlikely but by no means impossible, could leave shirt numbers standing well below 100 or well above 200. The best thing for a gambler to do is leave this alone, although a small flutter on the buy side could prove entertaining. The bookmakers do not have this luxury, and they cannot agree on what to do. Most set an opening price in the high 50s. Sporting Index takes a risk, and sets it at 49 to 52. They reason that Akinbiyi, who had scored just two league goals this season for his old side Leicester, will not score for Palace on his debut.

They are swamped by buyers. This is no surprise. The big risk is entirely on the upside. Who would sell at 60 – let alone 49 – when one player can put 110 on the board with two goals for his home team, and the other attackers may add 27 or 29 for every goal? If the match were to end 3–2, the make-up could be around 200. So selling could net you at most 60 points profit or potentially a 140-point loss (or worse). Most individual gamblers will shy away from the risk of enormous losses on an individual game, which is one way the bookies make their money.

The wave of buyers forces Sporting into an orderly retreat, pushing the price higher and higher until, shortly before kick-off, it is at 58 to sell, 60 to buy. 'Still no one is selling,' says a market-maker gloomily. He is contemplating Sporting's alarming exposure and admits, 'We're short of Shirt Numbers by more than two thousand pounds a point. A goal by Akinbiyi will cost us more than a hundred grand.'

The match itself produces moments of high drama. The game begins promisingly for those long of Shirt Numbers, when Sturridge (29), puts Wolves ahead in just the 13th minute. Akinbiyi has several good chances and gets a touch almost on the goal line during a mad scramble in the

Wolves penalty-box. A market-maker admitted later, 'Oh God, I remember that moment. We were terrified.' By some bizarre fluke the ball did not go in. The second half is a let down. Shaun Newton (20) gives Wolves a two-goal lead in the 65th minute, and there the scoring ends. Shirts make up at 49. Sporting had it right after all. Anyone who took a flutter and bought Shirt Numbers got plenty of entertainment. The sellers made money, but I doubt they had fun.

Betting on Shirt Numbers has two advantages over betting on Total Goals. The first is that the bookmaker's spread is small, usually just 3 or 4 points. That is a smaller percentage of the likely make-up than you get on Total Goals. The second is that because it is more volatile, value is more likely to lie in selling than buying. People, understandably, are terrified of selling Shirt Numbers because any individual game can produce huge losses. If you sell Total Goals, you have a good idea of your likely downside. Not so with Shirt Numbers, which can make up at zero or (on a wild night) in three figures.

This market is especially volatile on the upside. Flukes do happen: a substitute wearing number 37 who has barely scored all season can come on and net two goals. So the best times to sell are when there is a hefty margin between your calculations and the price. If your calculations suggest Shirt Numbers will make up at 23 in today's game, and the bookmaker is offering a price of 26 to 30, do not rush to sell at a hefty stake. The margin of difference is too narrow. If, in the above example, the bookies offer a price of 46 to 50, sell.

Shirt Numbers, like Multi-corners and Bookings, has traditionally attracted amateurs dreaming of the big score and warded off those afraid of a bad night. As a result the prices have, traditionally, been set too high and buyers massively outweighed sellers. This is changing. The punters are getting clever – sometimes too clever.

When Liverpool hosted Roma in the Champions League, the opening price for Shirt Numbers was 33 to 36 at IG. Sporting set it lower, at 29 to sell. They predicted that Michael Owen (number 10) would start, although his fitness was being tested at the time. Many agreed and flooded IG with bets, selling shirts at 33. They were wrong. Instead, Jari Litmanen began up front. His shirt number was 37. Within seven minutes he scored from the penalty spot. 'Everyone's done their Shirts in the seventh minute,' shouted Gary Hope, IG's market-maker, laughing. For once, the punters were short of the market and the book-makers were long. They cleaned up.

The market attracts insider dealing. Over drinks after the game, one IG market-maker told me, 'We have a client who usually knows what's going on inside the Liverpool locker room. This time he called us up shortly before the team was announced and sold Shirt Numbers. He thought Owen would start. He called back a few minutes later and wanted to void the bet. I told him the price hadn't moved. He could close the bet if he wanted, but he would have to pay the three-point spread.' Insider dealing on shares is illegal, but not on sports. You may or may not consider it unethical to gain an edge by using privileged informa-tion, but it's a bit much when the punter in question cries foul because his inside tip was wrong.

Notwithstanding the betting on the Roma game, it's an open secret that in these markets the long-term value has tended to lie on the sell side. The bookmakers have no reason to drop their prices while buyers are willing to pay over the odds. By selling, you simply help them carry the risk, absorbing some of their losses when the numbers soar. 'Before kick-off, seventy per cent of bets are buys,' says David Garbacz. 'They don't mind seeing a big seller at thirty-four, because all they've seen so far are buyers at thirty-eight.'

However, to make money over the long run, you have to stay at the table. Avoid getting wiped out by a single fluke. Keep your bets per point low and eke out profits.

Also, if you are looking to sell Shirt Numbers, wait until kick-off. The punters usually like to buy it, and the price might move higher, raising your margin and your potential profit. You might also gain an extra edge. Garbacz recalls, 'Sunderland were playing Newcastle. Sunderland had just signed Patrick Mboma from Parma. We had seen a clip on Sky. He was holding up shirt number seventy. We priced up the market at sixty-plus. The team came out, and he was wearing number seven. We saw a steady stream of sellers. Punters were paying attention. It took us a couple of minutes to work it out. Then we dropped the price in a hurry.'

Shirt Numbers can also reward the clever punter in other ways. Veteran punter John Hall looks at the numbers on the substitute bench as well as those starting on the field. 'Watch out for Shirt Numbers – you can get burned betting blind,' he says. 'But if you are watching on Sky there is time to see the teams and, more importantly, who's on the bench. They're using more and more subs now. I've made good money on Chelsea. They have higher numbers, particularly on the bench, where there's Zola and several others in the twenties. I bought Chelsea Shirt Superiority at six against Tottenham once and it made up, I think, at seventy-one. Gudjohnsen scored twice and he wears twenty-two. I went off to the races at Cheltenham with four thousand pounds.'

Coventry are playing Crystal Palace at Selhurst Park in a First Division match-up. Both sides are under-strength thanks to injuries and suspensions, and I reason the chances favour a low-scoring game. Palace midfielder Steve Thompson is out with an ankle injury, while Coventry are missing several players, including Lee Hughes, their top striker, who is finishing a four-match suspension, and Jairo Martinez, who has a knee injury.

The most obvious bet is to sell Total Goals, but the price is already low. Shirt Numbers looks a more attractive short at 35. Up front for Coventry is Jay Bothroyd, wearing number 21, but he has scored only four goals this season. Palace seem the likelier team to score, which will probably mean Morrison (10) and Freedman (9). I sell Shirt Numbers at 35 – and quickly regret it.

Jay Bothroyd duly opens the scoring for Coventry in the 12th minute. Before half-time the visitors make it 2–0. The second goal is scored by Coventry's number 3, Marcus Hall, so the total at the break is just 24, still well within profit. Luckily for me, Palace have had a goal disallowed for offside, while just before half-time an angry confrontation between Bothroyd and Palace's Danny Granville sees them both sent off. Granville wears number 30, so 51 points have just been removed from the pitch.

Palace play much better after the break and in the 57th minute Dougie Freedman makes it 2–1. The Shirts total is now 33. Much worse than that, however, is that more goals look distinctly possible, either from the sustained Palace pressure or from Coventry on the break. The game has a one-goal margin and with twenty men on the pitch it is wide open. Palace's Julian Gray, shirt number 24, is now looking like their most dangerous player. I am growing very uneasy. On the hour Coventry add 19 to the potential Shirt Numbers total by taking off Julian Joachim (number 10) and bringing on Gary McSheffrey (29). That's it, I'm out of here. The bookies have moved the Shirt Numbers price to 48 to 50. With twenty-five minutes to go I buy back my bet at 50, taking a painful, but survivable, 15-point loss. Ten minutes later Gary McSheffrey cheers me up by putting the ball in the back of the net to make it 3–1 to Coventry. Thank God I got out. The final make-up is 62. I have no material interest in the outcome at this point, but a loss avoided sometimes feels almost as good as a profit made. Selling out early saved me a further 12 points.

The bookmakers set the prices in a roundabout manner. They predict the number of goals each team is likely to score. Only then do they look at the likely scorers' shirt numbers, to produce a 'weighted average Shirt Number' per team. So they might say, 'We expect Liverpool to score two goals tonight. Michael Owen scores half of Liverpool's goals, so he will probably score one. He wears number ten. Add ten to the Shirt Numbers total,' and so on down the list. This total number will represent not the likely Shirt Numbers on a given night but what it would make up as an average after 1,000 typical games.

The bookmakers add the numbers together to produce the Shirt Numbers market. They then subtract the predicted loser's total from that of the expected winner to produce another market, Shirt Number Supremacy. This tortuous approach is heavily dependent on the initial forecast of how many goals each team is likely to score and so can often lead to some peculiar results.

Liverpool, flying high at the top of the Premiership, are at home to Fulham. Although Liverpool have just thumped Middlesbrough 2–0, Fulham have beaten Everton by the same score. Support for the Reds is nevertheless running strong and Liverpool are heavily favoured on Supremacy and the Win Index. As a result, the Scousers are given a hefty Shirt Number Supremacy of 12 to 15.

This, though, makes little sense. Although Liverpool

have the more prolific goal-scorers in Owen and Heskey, these players wear numbers 10 and 8. Meanwhile, Fulham's chief strikers are Barry Hayles (shirt 15) and Louis Saha (shirt 20). A goal each by Owen and Heskey will give a Liverpool Shirt Number tally of 18. But a single goal by either Hayles or Saha would knock that back to around zero. Hayles scored a double against Everton four days ago. If we assume the top strikers will score the goals, Liverpool have to outscore Fulham by roughly 2–1 simply to break even on Shirt Numbers.

Yet here the selling price is 12. That gives a pro-Fulham bet a huge head start. You sell Liverpool Shirt Supremacy, and this proves highly profitable, as the game produces a dull 0–0 draw. One game in eleven ends goalless, but Liverpool's two strikers would have had to produce an emphatic 2–0 result for you to lose money.

The Shirt Numbers markets attract inveterate gamblers because of their wild unpredictability. There is also a market (at Sporting) on the Aggregate Shirt Numbers in a particular set of games on any given Saturday. On the same day I looked at Winning Distances for Away Victories, the Shirts price for the same seven games was 275 to 285. As you would expect 18.2 goals in seven games, this implied an average shirt number per goal scorer of 15. Buying would have proved profitable, as the market made up at 323. That reflected a bumper crop of twenty-two goals, several scored by players wearing high numbers including Ipswich's Marcus Bent (number 38), Chelsea's John Terry (26), Derby's Branko Strupar (25), West Ham's Jermain Defoe (25) and a brace by Leicester's Paul Dickov (22). Even this rather remarkable set of occurrences produced a result only 13 per cent above the buy price of 285. As you should have gathered by now, this market is usually overpriced.

As in the cases of Akinbiyi and Owen, the Shirt Numbers markets attract a lot of attention because of the powerful role that can be played by an individual. Increasingly the spread firms are catering more directly to the same demand, by offering direct bets on the stars.

8

Hot Shots

IG Index lost a bundle in a few seconds when England played Greece for a place in the World Cup Finals in the autumn of 2001. David Beckham scored from one of his trademark spectacular free-kicks. It wasn't so much that he scored that did the damage. It was the fact that he did so in the 90th minute.

In spread betting you cannot place a direct bet on whether your favourite player will score. But you can bet on his Goal Minutes, on his chances of scoring the first or last goal, and on his overall performance.

Most bookies offer a market on Player Goal Minutes. IG, tipping its cap to Brian Clough, calls this market It Only Takes a Minute. The buy price for David Beckham in England's qualifier was 19. That meant IG thought Beckham would score once, around the 19th minute – or once in the 6th minute and once in the 13th (or, for that matter, nineteen times in the opening minute). I usually use the players Goal Minutes as a simple proxy for whether they will score. The average goal time is around 50 minutes, so Beckham's price equated to a 38 per cent chance of him scoring. A price of 12 to buy is roughly a

25 per cent chance. You can explore whether players tend to score early or late, or you can just translate the goal times into chances of scoring and take pot luck.

The likelier they think he is to score, obviously, the higher a player's price. IG set Beckham's price low to tempt in the punters. They were looking good, too, until that final free-kick. One fan bought Beckham's Goal Minutes at 15 at £300 a minute. He made £21,300.

Betting on individual players can be tremendous fun. It is also possible to find a good edge, if you have spotted an individual entering a purple patch before everyone else. Second-line scorers often offer better value to buy. The big-name strikers attract all the amateur money, and the bookmakers effectively have to underprice others so that the total market does not add up to too much.

Robert Pires was proving to be the magic man at Arsenal in the second half of the 2001/2 season, before injury cut his season short, but for a while everyone was still concentrating on Thierry Henry. It was clear to regulars at Highbury that Henry somewhat went off the boil in the second half of the season. The numbers tell the story: his average Goal Minutes, for games he started, was an amazing 56 before New Year's, but just 20 afterwards. For Pires the numbers were 14 and 23. Yet in February you could still buy his Goal Minutes at 12 while Henry was on 25. When Pires was injured, Freddie Ljungberg stepped into the attacking-midfielder gap and proved as good, or even better value. His second-half Goal Minutes would eventually average 33 a game. Yet he, too, was going cheap compared to Henry. At Manchester United, Ole Gunnar Solskjaer stepped on the pedal in the second half of the season but he was cheaper to buy than Van Nistelrooy, whose form, like Henry's, tailed off as the season progressed.

Experienced punter John Hall says, 'I've won quite a lot of money on Gudjohnsen at Chelsea because he can usually be bought around fifteen, whereas they usually put Hasselbaink higher, in the twenties or even the thirties. Danny Murphy at Liverpool is also quite a good buy. He's usually priced at around ten. You're often better off looking at one of the midfielders, rather than a name goal-scorer like Hasselbaink.'

Equally, if you spot a headline striker who is slowing down you could go short – though this would probably ruin your Saturday. Top-flight strikers, such as Henry, Ruud Van Nistelrooy, Alan Shearer and Michael Owen are worth buying into the thirties over the season (see Appendices, Table 17).

Sporting Index also offers a market called First-Last Blast. They give you 25 points if your chosen player scores the first goal of the match. They give you 25 if he scores the last goal. If he scores both, or the only goal, you get 50 points. If he does not score, or if his goal is sandwiched by others, it makes up at zero. Pires was routinely priced at just 6 to buy, compared to 18 for Henry. Pires's price seemed absurdly cheap, as indeed it proved on several occasions.

What you should pay in this market depends, of course, on how likely you think a particular player is to score. If he were guaranteed to score, the correct price would 24. This reflects the high number of 1–0 games, where his goal will count for 50 points. So players with a one-third chance of scoring should be worth up to 8 points, those with a one-quarter chance, 6 points.

For obvious reasons, the sell prices for FLB will add up to less than 50. If they rose above it, you could simply sell the lot and guarantee a profit. The bookmakers make their money on the spread. They may also make it by ramping up the prices on the most popular strikers, such as Ruud Van Nistelrooy and Thierry Henry. The Premiership's top goal-scorer last season, Henry, scored 24 goals in 32 starts, or 0.75 per game. So he was worth overall no more than 18 in First-Last Blast. The bookmakers must drop prices on others to keep the total below 50.

The prices, especially for favourites are largely set by English fans and these are not always best informed about overseas teams. Doing some research can pay dividends. For example, when Leverkusen came to England for a high-profile Champions League game, strikers Ulf Kirsten and Oliver Neuville were priced at 17 and 15 to buy in FLB. Michael Ballack was much cheaper, at just 12, even though he had been in terrific form. Why? Kirsten had scored for Leverkusen against an English team the previous week, and so was well known. Also, Ballack was a midfielder.

FLB is the cheapest way to bet on a goalless draw. The bookies offer a price for 'No Goal/Own Goal', which means you get 50 if there is no goal, or 25 if the first or the last goal is an own goal. Goalless draws occur 9 per cent of the time, equating in a 50 index to a price of 4.5. The price for No Goal/Own Goal is usually quoted at 6 to 8, which means you could, over time, make a profit by simply selling it, game in and game out. This will be dull, and expose you to some serious short-term losses. Alternatively you can avoid it until you think a goalless draw is much more likely than usual, and then buy.

There is a host of other markets on individual players, including player performances and bets on goals by a nominated group of players. Player performances vary from bookmaker to bookmaker, and suffer from the problem that they count all sorts of things, such as completed passes in the opposition half, which are almost impossible to keep track of accurately. Sporting Index's website includes a useful 'Results' archive, which shows the make-ups for past games. This allows you to see how individual players' performances have come out in different games, which can be a helpful guide. A market-maker there says: 'Attacking midfielders tend to get the highest ratings. David Beckham or Rivaldo usually make up in the 70s or 80s. Strikers tend to be lower, because they pass the ball to others less often.' Details matter in these markets. For example, Sporting gives points for successful passes in the opponents' half – but only the recipient need be past the halfway line for it to count.

Ipswich are playing Inter Milan in a UEFA Cup tie. Ipswich won the first leg at home 1–0, but they are faring poorly in the Premiership this season, and many argue they were very lucky in the first game.

Inter want revenge. As they have just been booted out of an Italian cup, they are particularly eager for a win and can be expected to go all out in attack. They also have the advantage of playing at home. After hunting around on the internet you find something interesting. Almost two-thirds of Inter Milan's goals come from two players. Mohammed Kallon and Christian Vieri have scored thirteen of the team's twenty-one goals this season. Inter will be relying on the big two to win the match.

Yet IG Index is offering something called the 'Shooting Stars' market at just 24 to 27. For this they list four key players, two per side. Each time one of them scores, you get 20 points. If any does not play at all, you get 5 points as consolation. Tonight the named players include Inter's two top goal-scorers, Kallon and Vieri, as well as Pablo

Counago and Finidi George from Ipswich. If Inter are
going on the attack, at home, against a weak team, you
have to assume their two top strikers will score at least
one between them. So that gets you to 20 points straight
off. Anything above that moves you into profit. You buy
at 27 at £10 a point. In effect you are putting down £270.
Every time a nominated player scores, you get £200 back.

The game begins wonderfully. Ipswich's Counago is
left on the bench. We didn't expect him to score anyway,
and as long as he is not brought on later as a substitute
we will get 5 points, worth £50, back. Players must take
no part at all to collect the consolation. After kick-off
Ipswich have a brief moment of possession and then Inter
take control. Kallon and Vieri dominate and in the 18th
minute Vieri scores. You are now on 25 points. So you
have already got £250 back, leaving you £20 out of the
money so far with more than seventy minutes to go. Still
Inter press, and fifteen minutes later Vieri puts in another
and Ipswich start to crumble. The game is barely half an
hour old and you are already well into profit, with nothing
but the possibility of more money to come. The make-up
so far is 45 – two goals and a no show. As you bought at
27 at £10, you are already sitting on £180 profit.

In the second half it gets even better. Kallon scores
moments after the break. Hot Shots for the evening now
stands at 65, £380 profit. Fifteen minutes later you start
booing when Counago is seen warming up on the sidelines, before he is brought on as a substitute – for George.
This is the worst of all possible worlds, because you lose
the 5 points you expected for Counago's no-show, while
George's early exit removes one of the four players who
can increase your profit by scoring. Hot Shots has now
fallen back to 60. Ten minutes later, Vieri makes your
evening complete by scoring his third. He and Kallon

provide extra entertainment by producing some good chances, each of which would have netted you a further £200 if it had found the net, but your remarkable run of good luck is exhausted. The final make-up is 80. You bought at 27, so your profit is £530.

All Hot Shots markets are not exactly the same. Sporting Index, Cantor and Spreadex all offer 25 points for a goal and 8 for a no-show. IG is holding out alone with a different index. Sporting and Spreadex call it 'Hot Shots', Cantor, 'Netbusters'. Some, such as IG, allow you to trade it in running. Crucially, the bookmakers sometimes offer different players. *Racing Post* each morning will have details. It takes a lot of work to look across the full range of markets, from Goals to Shirt Numbers to Hot Shots and Players' Goal Minutes, before a match. But the better your knowledge of the teams, the better your opportunity to gain an edge.

Bayer Leverkusen are at home to Arsenal in a Champions League fixture, and the signs suggest a goalfest. Both teams are among the most prolific attackers in European football. In Neuville, Kirsten and Ballack, Leverkusen have three star goal-scorers. Arsenal's Henry, possibly the best striker in the world, is on good form. Add in a Gunners back row that looks like a M*A*S*H unit – Adams and Keown are among the wounded – and goals seem highly likely. There are several ways to play. The bet might be on Total Goals, scorers' Shirt Numbers, Total Goal Minutes, Hot Shots or the Goal Minutes of individual goal-scorers. You might even bet on the timing of the goals. The question is where you find the best value.

Total Goals are offered at 2.9 to buy. This means you need four goals to make real money. That happens in just 27 per cent of Premiership matches, and in recent years in 25 per cent of second-round Champions League games. This is unappealing. Shirt Numbers are priced at 41 to buy. Neuville is wearing 27. This looks better. However, Kirsten wears an unhelpful 9, and Ballack is only slightly more useful at 13. Henry, perhaps the likeliest scorer on either side, wears 14, Sylvain Wiltord number 11, and Dennis Bergkamp 10. The average for these six is 14. If they were equally likely to score, that would make a Shirts price of 41 the equivalent to 2.9 goals. Total Goal Minutes will cost 145 to buy. The average goal time is 50 minutes, so that is also the equivalent of 2.9 goals. This is not surprising, because that is how they usually work out the numbers, but it is worth checking.

Turn instead to the markets on individual goal-scorers. At Spreadex, for example, Hot Shots is offered at 36 to buy. They give 25 points per scorer, and 8 for a no show. The nominated players are Neuville, Kirsten, Henry and Wiltord. The other bookmakers offer the same players at the same prices. This looks more attractive. The first three are likeliest to score. The price, 36, is equivalent to 1.44 goals. Or, to put it more simply, two goals from this group will put you into serious money (50 points, for a 14-point profit).

Compare that to the prices for these players in their individual Goal Minutes markets. The buy prices are Neuville 23, Kirsten 17, Henry 21 and Wiltord 14. In total that makes 75. With the average goal timed at 50 minutes, that equates to 1.5 goals. However, and this is critical, Wiltord seems far less likely to score than the other three. Hot Shots throws him into the pot for free, as it were. We can buy the Goal Minutes of Neuville, Kirsten and Henry for just 61 minutes – or 1.22 times the average goal time. This is the cheapest bet. We buy the Goal Minutes of all three players.

The game proved a dull washout in many ways, not least because of the driving rain that hampered the attacks. The pace was sluggish. Robert Pires scored for Arsenal, but that is no help to us. (It was this game that started me betting on Pires, with profitable results later.) The bet seemed a loss-maker until the 90th minute – when Ulf Kirsten scored after a fabulous cross into the box from the right wing. The final result was 1–1.

Had you bet on Total Goals, you would have lost 0.9 points. As one would bet quite heavily per point, this would have resulted in some painful losses. Shirt Numbers, priced at 41 to buy, made up at a measly 16, a thumping loss. Total Goal Minutes made up just in profit at 146. Hot Shots, priced at 36, made up at 25 for a small loss. But Goal Minutes for the three players chosen made up at 90 – thanks to Kirsten. Neuville and Henry made up at zero, but we don't care. The profit is 29, or almost exactly half the 61-point stake we risked.

Of course, luck plays a huge part. The match could easily have gone in several other directions. Henry was fouled when through on goal. Both sides missed easy chances. The key goal came very late. On the whole, we were unlucky to see so few goals. But buying the cheapest market turned a potential hefty loss into a juicy profit.

Player Goal Minutes should be bought selectively. They are expensive. You are paying a three-minute spread per player. Each one is also apt to be slightly overpriced for two reasons. First, by its nature a market in, say, Teddy Sheringham's Goal Minutes will attract those who fancy Sheringham to have a good match rather than those who think he will do poorly. The pro-Sheringham money will drive the price. Second, sellers carry huge risk. Selling Sheringham's Goal Minutes at 11 at £10 a point offers a maximum profit of £110. If he scores in the ninetieth minute, you will lose £790. Heaven help you if he scores a hat-trick.

There are occasional opportunities to buy Total Goal Minutes for the match and sell the players' individual Goal Minutes. You would need to use Sporting Index because it offers Goal Minutes on many more players; for big games it will offer prices on eighteen. Sometimes this seems to offer an opportunity for arbitrage, when the combined sell prices of the players' Goal Minutes add up to more than the price for the Total Goal Minutes. Obviously, it is impossible for those players to score more goals, at whatever time, than are scored overall in the game. That would leave you guaranteed to pocket the difference between the two, plus the minutes of any goals scored by substitutes or those not listed. As I have a peculiar fondness for the idea of free money I took a closer look at this. Alas, the arbitrage is almost invariably illusory. Usually four or five of the listed players will not start, so the bets are void. But going long–short, buying TGM and selling Minutes for the individual players, is not as silly as it might sound. It becomes, in effect, a bet on the Goal Minutes of those players not listed, such as defenders and substitutes.

When Leeds hosted Man U, Total Goal Minutes was 145 to buy, while the Goal Minutes of the eighteen listed players added up to 152 to sell. The latter dropped to 99 when five players, including Van Nistelrooy, Forlan and Bowyer, did not start. This seemed to promise a 46-point loss. However, in the event this bet would have turned a good profit.

When listed players do not start you are short of the Goal Minutes of a smaller number of players. There are more players on the pitch who will net you a profit on TGM, where you are long, without costing you money on player Goal Minutes, where you are short. In the above example, your salvation came in the unlikely form of Lee Bowyer. He did not start, voiding the bet against his Goal Minutes (at 6). Yet he came on as a sub and scored in the 80th minute. Total Goal Minutes for the game added up to 302 as it ended 4–3 to Manchester. Overall profit from the two bets was 34 points.

If that sounds complicated, aren't you glad you're not a hedge fund? These secretive speculative operations do this sort of thing on the stock market every day. At the time of writing a growing number of people think hedge funds walk on water. They are making money and causing mayhem going short of the likes of Vodafone and Japanese Government Bonds, performing complicated double or triple somersaults between financial institutions. It will end in tears. Long Term Capital Management, the mother of all hedge funds, ended up needing a £2.5 billion bailout by the big banks.

Betting on individual players can be hugely entertaining, and – maybe – profitable. But if you are going to do detailed research, the long-term markets might offer the best value of all. These allow bets on who will win the Premiership, the World Cup, the Champions League or Serie A. Trading in running is easy, and can take place over weeks or months rather than minutes. And if you are on your toes, and you can spot teams on the way up or down before anyone else, there is good money to be made.

9

Long-term Markets

Half time at Highbury on a mild January afternoon, and an old friend looms out of the crowd and tugs at my sleeve. We haven't seen each other in five years, so of course we immediately start talking about football. Manchester United, after an awful autumn, are riding high again at the top of the table and he is shaking his head about the missed betting opportunity: 'Do you realise you could have bought Man U at ten to one to win the Premiership,' he says. 'I could have put a hundred quid on them.'

If you'd put £100 on Man U at 10–1, you'd have lost £100. The Red Devils cruised for three months and then staggered through a handful of surprise losses, including defeats at home to Liverpool and more amazingly, Middlesbrough, which left them with a mountain to climb. They finished third.

Pity the fixed odds punter. He has to pick the winner. In the spreads you make money if your team simply does better than expected. The bookmakers offer long-term markets on almost every competition, including the Premiership and the other English leagues, the other major European domestic leagues, the FA Cup, Champions

League and international tournaments such as the World
Cup. Prices move to reflect fortunes on the field, but you
can trade in and out.

It is early December and Manchester United are deep
in their losing trough, dropping four games out of six,
which leaves them struggling in seventh position. They
have just 21 points from 14 games. Yet a look at the
simplest market, for Premiership Points, shows something
curious. People still believe. 'You can never write them
off' as half the phone-in callers are saying on the radio.
The Premiership Points market allows you to bet on the
total number each team is likely to win over the season.
At this moment Man U are 71.5 to buy, 70 to sell. If you
buy at 71.5 and United finish with more than that, you
make money.

This price is high. On the field Liverpool are 8 points
ahead with a game in hand, but in the spreads they are
priced to finish just 4.5 points better; Aston Villa have 3
points more than United so far and they are priced at 56;
Everton are 1 point behind United, but their price is 46.
Certainly you should pay more for quality, but how much
more? Chelsea are 2 points ahead of Manchester, but you
can buy their Premiership points for 63.5.

Football pundits and bar-room bores talk about teams
having so many points 'with a game (or two) in hand'.
This is not helpful for a spread better. The best way to
compare performances to date is to look at points won per
game. So far United have collected just 1.5. This is poor
stuff. Spurs and Villa have more; Liverpool have 2.23 per
game.

Gary Lineker is in the papers, arguing United will
bounce back. He argues that any manager who can leave
David Beckham on the bench for several weeks, as Sir
Alex Ferguson is doing, has an unmatchable pool of talent

to draw from. It's a strong argument, but United have to do more than bounce back. At the rate of 1.5 points a game they are on track to end the season with 57 points. To make the 71.5 price at the bookmakers, they need to win just over 2 points a game from here.

That is a championship-winning season. The team winning the Premiership in the previous five years has collected the following number of points per game over the season: 2.16, 1.97, 2.05, 2.08, 2.39 and 2.11. Can United do this? Of course. But does that seem the likeliest outcome? The team has just lost 3–0 at home to Chelsea, 3–1 at Arsenal, 3–1 at Liverpool and even 2–1 at home to lowly Bolton. Players are pointing fingers at one another in the papers. Fabien Barthez seems to be having one of his turns a week. Possibly sparking the collapse, and certainly contributing to it, is Sir Alex Ferguson's well-trailed plan to retire at the end of the season. Speculation over his replacement is dominating the back pages. I am always looking for a chance to sell United, which is generally overpriced. At 70, the sell price, it is tempting.

A look ahead at the schedule suggests waiting. In midweek the team faces an easy Champions League fixture, at home against Boavista. A good result there will bring the United believers out in force. They will seize on any good news as the sign that the team is over the worst and the market has bottomed out. The price will rise. So it proves: United trounce Boavista 3–0 and in the Premiership Points markets their price leaps to 72 to sell, 73.5 to buy. I sell.

Profits appear quickly. United initially carry on losing at home, and even the believers start to entertain doubts. After United lose 1–0 at home to West Ham the price in Premiership Points falls to a low of 67 to sell, 68.5 to buy.

Having sold at 72, I can now buy the bet back at 68.5 and collect a clear 35-point profit. But the price still looks too high given the team's recent form. I hold on for a more dramatic fall.

You can be wrong and make a mint, and you can be right and lose money. In this case I did the latter. United bounced back, winning eight league games on the trot and leaping to the head of the table by late January, when they began to assume an aura of invincibility. It was my worst-case scenario. But my losses were minimal. Why?

The price barely moved in the Points market. Despite this extraordinary recovery United, which I sold at 72, could still be bought back for 75.5. This shows how far the price in early December had already anticipated most of the recovery. If an amazing comeback does not move the price much, then the initial price was too high. I bought my bet back for a loss. They finished the season with 77 points.

While I was losing money on the headline story, sharper-eyed punters were collecting juicy profits further down the table. During the same two months Newcastle's price soared. Early in December, while Man U were priced for perfection, the Magpies were going cheap. They had won 1.71 points per game so far, but were priced to get no more than 1.4 for the rest of the season. They had 24 points, 3 more than Manchester, but you could buy their Season Points for just 57. Why was this?

Newcastle had a thinner talent pool than those of some rivals. It was reasonable to expect that their form would weaken. But the team also suffers from southern snobbery. Most spread betters are still from the southeast. When they think of Newcastle at all they think of Jimmy Nail. The team also suffers from football snobbery. Captain Alan Shearer was seen as yesterday's man, linked in most people's eyes with Kevin Keegan's abysmal reign as England manager. Sir Bobby Robson, the Newcastle manager, also seemed too English and dull compared to the clever, glamorous Europeans managing further south.

December was to prove a superb month as Newcastle won five games, including victories at Arsenal and Leeds. They had their fair share of luck, for instance benefiting from Ray Parlour's sending off at Highbury. By Boxing Day their price had raced to 66.5 to buy, 65 to sell, for an 8-point profit.

At these junctures it is tempting to take your profits by selling the bet back. It is often right to do so. The rise in the price suggests that much of the quick momentum trade has already taken place. For further profits you find yourself in for the long haul. I'm an inveterate profit-taker. I like cash. But others take a different view. Most importantly, Newcastle still looked cheap. They were now at the head of the Premiership, yet United, Arsenal, Liverpool and Leeds were much more expensive. Newcastle, with 39 points from 19 games, had won 2.05 points per game. To make the price they still had to win just 1.45 a game for the rest of the season. The market expected Spurs (1.55) and Fulham (1.48) to do better. Even Sunderland were expected to do almost as well – their price, 52 to buy, demanded 1.37 points per game. So far, 13 points behind their northeastern rivals, that is all they had achieved.

The following month was less successful. Although Newcastle beat Leeds, Tottenham and Bolton, they also suffered losses against Manchester United and Chelsea, and even drew with Leicester. By month's end their price was barely moved at 67 to buy. This was a clearer sign to sell. The momentum had gone, United were back on top. Newcastle's record by now had fallen to 1.8 points per game, the price expected 1.6 for the 15 games left.

They finished the season fourth with 71 points. Villa and Spurs, incidentally, finished eighth and ninth with 50 points each and Fulham thirteenth with 44. Sunderland just avoided relegation with 40 points.

The bookmakers extend this type of long-term or aggregate market across major tournaments and into different sports. You can buy or sell a team's Total Goals, Corners, Bookings and Goal Minutes for the Champions League or World Cup. You can also trade the totals for the entire tournament. The same principles apply. Going into the 2002 World Cup, England's Total Corners was 22 to sell, 24 to buy. The average is five per game, so that anticipated England would play between four and five matches and be knocked out in either the last sixteen or the quarter-finals.

More and more of these markets are springing up almost daily. To set your baseline, you need to start with basic per-match averages, which is how the bookmakers create their original prices. The data you need can often be found on websites such as Soccerbase and Opta. Then take a view.

Even more popular are the long-term indices. These offer more action – and more risk. The bookmakers make you a deal. They'll give you £60 if United win the title; £40 if they come second; £30 if they come third; £20 for fourth; £10 for fifth; and £5 for sixth. How much would you pay up front to take this bet? This is a 60 Index, giving 60 points for the winner, 40 for second place and so on. As with all Index markets, there is a strict maximum number of points you can win or lose, so you control your exposure.

In early December, when United's Premiership Points were priced at 68.5, they fell as low as 28 in the

Championship Index. Buy them at £100 a point and you risk £2,800. If they come third you get £3,000 back, a small profit. If they come second you get £4,000. If they win you get £6,000. If they don't place, you lose your stake.

Even though they were ninth in the league, the market priced them to come either fourth, collecting 20 points, or third, collecting 30. Here was the buying opportunity for bulls. A United comeback would produce a bigger jump in the price than in the points market, for two reasons. First, the Points Price was already too high. Second, an index is more leveraged. Small changes in form can produce huge changes in price. The index can be better for in-running traders because these big movements make it easier to cover the spread – assuming you bet correctly.

As United recovered and started winning, bulls charged and sent the price soaring. Two months later you could sell your bet back for 45, nearly a 20-point rise from the bottom. During the same time Newcastle, whose points price rose from 57 to 65, saw their index price more than double. They were 13 to buy in early December and 28 to sell in January. This still left them priced to come just fourth. There is a school of thought that advises selling back enough to cover your initial bet so that no matter what happens you do not lose money. In this case, if you had bought Newcastle at 13 at £10 a point you could now sell £5 a point at 28. This would leave you slightly ahead, even if Newcastle imploded over the rest of the season and failed to come in the top six.

Like all spreads, indices work both ways. You can bet against a team by selling them, as well as betting for them by buying. You can even play the indices off against the fixed odds market. This is not as complicated as it sounds. Imagine you put £100 on Man U at 10–1 in your local betting shop in November. Now, in late January, you can use the spreads to close out your bet and collect some profit, by selling United at 45 in the index. You will make money on this bet if they come second (40 points) or below. And of course you will make money from your fixed bet if they win. It's a two-way play, what Jonathan Sparke calls 'the perfect round-trip', and what the City calls arbitrage.

You have to get the stakes right. Working it out takes a pencil and the back of a decent-sized envelope. In the above case, your fixed odds bet will return £1,000 profit if United win the title. If you sell in the index at 45, you will lose 15 points if that happens. Divide the £1,000 by 15 and you can afford to lose £66.67 a point. If you sell at that level in the index, you will break even if United win and will make a profit if they don't. If you sell for slightly less, you make a profit both ways.

All that depends on taking the right flyer at the right point in the season. Naturally, it will not always come off. It probably won't come off most of the time. Later in the same season Newcastle were offered at 40–1 to win the Premiership, even though they were only a handful of points behind in a tight race and had by far the easiest schedule. The odds were ludicrously long. I took the bet on the off-chance it would come in handy. A few good games, and one or two upsets elsewhere, and you would get the chance to close out for a tidy profit in the index. If you play it off against the spreads, you don't need your team to win – only move into second place. (No such luck – that time.)

For these opportunities you need two things. First, the odds have to be very long. You need big potential winnings in your back pocket before you can go heavily short without risk. It is possible to arbitrage using shorter-odds bets, but it is complex and the profits are likely to be minimal. Second, the team in question needs to be able to get itself into second place. Your fixed odds bet is on winning. That is the only eventuality it covers. If you then go short of a team in third place, you will be exposed if it finishes second. You will lose money on the short *and* get back nothing from the betting shop.

The index firms are now index crazy. There are markets available on all the main tournaments and English, Scottish and continental leagues, and on such things as who will be relegated from the Premiership and who will win the Golden Boot.

Three events took place in February 2002 that provided a ticket to profits for anyone quick on their feet. The first was that Arsenal drew with Newcastle in their first FA Cup quarter-final match. The second was that Arsenal lost to Juventus and went out of the Champions League. The third was that Manchester United suffered a surprise defeat against Middlesbrough that effectively ended their hopes of winning the Premiership. These three events meant you should sell Ruud Van Nistelrooy, at the time the highest goal-scorer in the league, in the Golden Boot competition. Why?

Arsenal's Thierry Henry was already on twenty goals, just one behind Van Nistelrooy. Henry was serving a three-match suspension for an earlier red card, but the Newcastle game used up one of those without damaging his Premiership goal-scoring chances. The rematch counted as a second one. He would, as a result, miss just one further game. Meanwhile, Arsenal's exit from the Champions League meant Henry would not have to be rested for any European matches. Finally, Man U's loss to Middlesbrough relieved Sir Alex Ferguson of the need to give the Premiership his all. He could now focus on

Europe. As a result Van Nistelrooy was rested ahead of the big clashes with Deportivo and Leverkusen. Even when he played, he was either substituted early or brought on late as a sub himself for a warm-up. Meanwhile, Henry and Chelsea's Jimmy-Floyd Hasselbaink, the other contender for the title, were going all out every game.

When these events occurred, Van Nistelrooy was 45 to sell in the Golden Boot Index at Sporting, which gives 60 points for the winner and 40 for the player in second place. Three weeks later, when United's exit from the Champions League suggested closing the bet, you could buy him back at 36, a fat 9-point profit.

Prices in these markets tend to move mechanically, in line with goal-scoring to date, and they can be slow to anticipate events. The markets offer good opportunities to bet against the best-known players. Punter John Hall says, 'I've tended to sell rather than buy. I would sell Michael Owen because you know he's going to miss a number of games through injury or being rested.' Owen's opening price will also reflect popular enthusiasm.

One downside to long-term betting is that it tends to use up a lot of your deposit, or credit limit, at the book-maker's. If you buy Man U's points at 70 at £1,000 a point at the start of the season, the bookmaker will – unbeliev-ably – want to see evidence you have £70,000, just in case United get no points at all. It ends up limiting your stake. Sometimes on the phone they will be reasonable, but you cannot depend on it.

With four games to go in the season, Derby look a clear sell in IG's Relegation Index. There is no realistic chance they will catch Ipswich, who are four points ahead in third-to-bottom place. Derby's schedule is grim: home to Newcastle, away to Liverpool, home to Leeds and away to Sunderland. The best they can reasonably hope for is three points, with draws against Newcastle, Leeds and Sunderland. Liverpool are still chasing the title and will surely not lose at home.

This index gives zero points for the team that comes bottom, 10 for second from bottom, 25 for third and 50 each for those that stay up.

Derby are priced at 11 to sell, though they seem certain to make up at 10. By selling you are trying to snatch a single point off the bookmakers. You sell for £100 a point. Derby collect just one more point, drawing at Sunderland in the final match of the season, and finish second from bottom. Ipswich won one, lost three and ended six points clear.

Taking a point from the bookies is possible surprisingly often. But there are big risks involved if you get it wrong. Had Derby produced a string of upsets and overtaken Ipswich they would have made up at 25. Selling at 11 at £100 a point would have cost £1,400. 'There is a temptation to think you're just buying money,' says John Hall. His biggest loss came from trying to do just that. The sport was golf, the competition long forgotten. 'The golfer was five strokes clear in the back nine. He was priced at nineteen in the Win Index, where they give twenty-five points for the winner. I dove in and bought at five hundred pounds a point. Then the ball went into the water.'

Indices vary. Sometimes the bookies give 100 points for the winner, sometimes 80, sometimes 60. Even those offering the same points for the winner can have different schedules. One 60 index for the Premiership gives points for all places down to number eight. Others stop at six. There are nasty pitfalls here for the unwary. All four big firms offered 100 indices for the World Cup. No two were the same. Each one gave different points further down the table: some gave 20 points for a team making the last sixteen, others gave just 10; some gave 33 points for quarter-finalists, others 25. You need to check very carefully before betting or you will lose money unnecessarily. Buying anything in an index is not about picking the winner, it is about accumulating points. A winning purchase at one firm can be a losing one at another.

This is the best reason for having accounts with several firms. Buying at the best price makes a big difference to long-term profits in spread betting. It is one of the ways professionals make their money.

All eyes are on the world's greatest football team. Real Madrid (2002 vintage) are cruising in the Champions League. They have sewn up their group with a perfect record so far, winning three out of three. They will collect 25 points for winning the group, and they are priced at 25. But there is still value to be had lower down the table. The unheralded Greek team Panathinaikos have leapt into second place following a surprise 2–0 victory over Sparta in Prague. Porto are apparently locked in the caboose with one point.

You can buy Panathinaikos at 8 in the Group Index. Second place collects 10 points, third place 5, so the upside is only 2 points. But the chances of getting it are huge so you can bet big stakes. The downside is minimal.

Panathinaikos are three points clear with three games left, two of them at home. Their remaining away fixture is to a demoralised Porto. They have already made their hopeless trip to the Bernabeu. Sparta, struggling to catch up, still have that treat ahead of them. The only plausible way the Czech team can hope to catch up is if they win the return match against Panathinaikos in Athens. A draw would not do, leaving Panathinaikos a point ahead with two games to go and a much easier run.

There is an easy way to ensure profits. You buy

Panathinaikos at 8 at £50 a point. If they come third you lose £150. If they come second, as you expect, you win £100. But you then place a fixed odds bet against them in the match against Sparta. The Czechs, playing away, are offered at a very juicy 11–2. You bet £28, and you have made a perfect round-trip. If Panathinaikos win the game they will lock up second place in the table and you collect £100 on the spreads. The £28 handed over in your local betting shop still leaves you £72 to the good. But if Sparta by some fluke win the game, that fixed odds bet will give you £154 profit. That will cover the £150 at risk in your spread bet, and let you buy a buy a pint to drown your sorrows. And even then it isn't over. Panathinaikos would still have the better chance to come second. That bet is for free.

It does not get much more complicated than this. Hours of hard work comparing prices and odds can leave you financially in a position as delicate and tangled as an illustration in the advanced section of the *Kama Sutra*. Bizarre potential dangers threaten. Panathinaikos, Sparta and Porto could end up all jockeying for second place, if Porto beat Real Madrid and the game in Prague is drawn. Be warned: even 'free' money isn't free. No matter how thoroughly you think you have thought it out, you will suddenly grow alarmed at an unlikely outcome. This usually happens just after you've gone to bed.

Panathinaikos beat Sparta 2–1 and finished second, two points clear of third place, even though they lose away to Porto. I lost my £28 fixed odds bet, but pocketed £100 from the spread.

A similar bet beckoned on the last weekend of the Six Nations rugby tournament. Wales had to beat Scotland in Cardiff to secure fourth position. You could buy Wales at 8 in the index, where fourth place secured 10 points, fifth place 5. Scotland, meanwhile, were given long odds to win the match. It was straightforward to buy Wales in the index and bet on Scotland to win the match. I was covered for everything except a draw. That almost never happens in rugby. But at night it suddenly seemed the likeliest outcome and I could calculate my risk to the penny. Scotland won 27–22.

These opportunities emerge when you have two separate chances to bet, effectively, on the same thing. Scotland winning the match (at one price) was the same as Scotland coming fourth in the tournament (at another price).

It is a famous night at Anfield, where Liverpool surprise the doubters by beating mighty Roma 2–0 to take the Italians' place in the final stages of the Champions League. Before the game they were given no chance. Now they are being talked up for a semi-final berth against Manchester United.

The first stage of the quarter-finals goes according to the patriot's script. Man U stun their Spanish opponents, Deportivo La Coruña, by winning the first leg in Spain, 2–0. Goals scored away count for extra, so they will go through unless the Spaniards score a major upset in the second leg at Old Trafford. Meanwhile, Liverpool play host to Bayer Leverkusen, the dark horses from Germany, and win the first leg 1–0 at Anfield. But they are a strong sell at 32 in a 60 index for the tournament. If they are knocked out by Leverkusen, they make up at 20. If they go out in the semi-final, they make up at 30. Only if they make the final do you face losses. The runner-up collects 40 points, the winner 60. The price offered is absurd. Only if they beat Leverkusen and then beat Man U in the semi-final will you lose money.

Liverpool travel to the BayArena for the second game

with a slim advantage, that single goal scored at home. Leverkusen are strong at home, where their record this season is 13–1–1. They have conceded 10 goals here in 15 games, or 0.67 per match, while scoring 43, or nearly 3 per game. The latter figure includes some near humiliations of major Bundesliga rivals, such as the 4–0 crushing of Dortmund. This is a huge contrast to their form away, where they are 7–4–4 with 30 goals for and 23 conceded. (The home-field advantage for major English and European teams is shown in the Appendices, Tables 7–10.)

I sell Liverpool. This seems more attractive than buying Leverkusen, then priced at 25 to buy, because there are two ways to play. Even if Liverpool win they have to face Man U before you start losing. But if you buy Leverkusen and Liverpool win, you lose straight away. And if Leverkusen win, their price is not likely to rise very far. The market will not give them much chance against Manchester United in the next round. Selling the team you expect to lose has an extra advantage over buying the likely winner. The loser makes up as soon as it goes out, allowing you to take your profits quickly without paying a second spread.

The game in the BayArena is wonderful. There are four goals in the second half, six in total. The lead flips back and forth between the two teams. Michael Owen misses some easy chances, but so do the home strikers. Klaus Toppmoller, the Germans' coach, provides his own spectacle. When I first saw him on the sidelines, I thought he was Norman Stone in a Harpo Marx wig, though after a moment I reluctantly conceded this was unlikely. Whenever his team goes ahead he leaps in the air and waves his arms. Whenever they surrender the lead he hunches on the bench and sucks down cigarettes in a single breath. His ticker has a tough night.

With fifteen minutes left Leverkusen are trying to

defend a 3–1 lead. At this point you can in theory lock in some profits on your bet against Liverpool by selling Leverkusen's Supremacy at 1.8, though I always struggle to do the sums quickly enough. The Germans finally win 4–2, giving them a 4–3 victory on aggregate and a berth in the semi-finals.

Oh, and the cards flew. That, too, was predictable. Portuguese referee Vitor Pereira was tough, both teams were going all out, and there was no love lost between them anyway. But I already had a bet on the outcome and I didn't want to watch two markets. Bookings were 36 to buy beforehand, and made up at 50. Most of them came in the second half, so you could have bought late in the first, predicting a scrappy final forty-five minutes, and been well in the money.

That bet closed successfully, the Champions League semi-finals are now sorted out. Manchester United will play Leverkusen, and Real Madrid are against Barcelona. Real and United stand out. Barca have had an indifferent season this year, and it is hard to see them overcoming Madrid over two legs. United, too, are in strong form. Exits from the FA Cup and two surprise defeats in the Premiership have left Sir Alex Ferguson's huge ambitions focused squarely on Europe. That the final will take place in Glasgow, his home town, is icing on the cake for him.

Leverkusen are Cinderella at the ball. She often makes it, but she rarely leaves with the Prince. It is almost their first major tournament performance since they were founded a century ago. Although United have lost both Beckham and Keane to injury, this did not stop them turning over Deportivo 5–2 on aggregate. Deportivo are a good team, who came to Highbury and beat Arsenal 2–0. The final looks likely to be Real–Man U.

Then there emerges something extraordinary. You can

have a nearly free bet. Here I moved from the 60 index, which had offered the best prices for the earlier round, to a 100 index offered at Sporting. This gave 100 points for the winner of the tournament, 75 for the runner-up and 50 for the losing semi-finalists.

Real are priced at 75 to buy, United at 74. If you buy both teams, you are paying 149 points. If they make up the finalists, you get 175 back. That is the likeliest scenario, and what you are betting on.

If only one goes through, you will almost certainly get your money back. Real should beat Leverkusen in the final; similarly, you'd expect United to see off Barcelona. The winner would collect 100 points, the losing semi-finalist 50, returning 150 points from a 149 bet. The only outcome where you lose money is if Real and United both lose in the semis, or one of them goes through and then loses to the heavy underdog in the final. You take that risk and buy both teams.

And then, of course, the facts get in the way of a good theory. Manchester United, as everyone says, are a superb team on paper. But I have never seen anyone play football on paper. On grass they were rubbish. Against Leverkusen they played far below their level, while the Germans played well above theirs. For all that, the scores ended level after both games. Leverkusen went through because they scored more away goals.

At this point you can still exit the bet for a small loss. The market is now making the same calculation that you made earlier about Real's likely chances against Leverkusen. Real are now priced at 90 to 92 in the 100 index. You can sell them back for a 10-point loss. You hold on and Real win the final 2–1, decided by an extraordinary strike late in the first half by Zinedine Zidane. You get your money back.

The bet did not work out but I would take it again every time it was offered, and most of the time it would be. One of the many advantages of spread betting is that you can buy more than one team in a competition. Multiple buys are a good way of looking for value in a crowded field, especially if you can find teams whose fortunes are likely to be interrelated. They do not offer the same spectacular returns as long shots, but they might offer better value. Make the quirks of the index work for you.

The bookmakers swear this never happened, but a City friend insists that he made £10,000 from the spread firms on the 1992 General Election when they made a critical error. They offered prices on the number of seats to be won by Labour, the Conservatives and the Liberal Democrats that added up to the total number of seats in Parliament, less a few for the Welsh and Scottish Nationalists. But they had forgotten about Northern Ireland, where the three main parties do not compete. As a result the friend was able to sell the seats totals for all three parties, guaranteeing huge profits. He recalled his conversation on the phone with the bookmaker. First he sold the Conservatives' total number of seats. The dealer happily took the order, thanked him and prepared to hang up. 'Hold on,' the friend said, 'I also want to sell Labour.' There was a pause. The dealer, surprised, took the order. The friend then said, 'And I also want to sell the Lib Dems.' There was a long pause. The dealer, baffled, asked, 'So who do you think is going to win?'

Election night proved even better than expected. Plaid Cymru, the Welsh nationalist party, scored a surprise upset in one seat in Wales – reducing the big three parties' seat count even further, and adding another £2,000 to my friend's profits. While, officially, the bookies deny this could ever have happened, one senior source confided to me, 'It could have been us. We were pretty naïve back then.'

It is a feature of any index that there are only so many points on offer. These days no spread firm will make the sell prices add up to more than the possible total, or the buy prices add up to fewer. But it is worthwhile counting up the prices. Bulls and bears are created equal, but that is not how they are treated.

The bookmakers all run indices for the FA Cup. By the time the tournament reached the last sixteen the sell prices at IG for the teams remaining added up to 370. The buy prices added up to 311. Yet there were only 380 points left on offer, from 80 for the winner to 10 for those destined to go out. If you sold every team you would lose £10; if you bought every team you would lose three times as much. The bias, as usual, lay on the downside. That is where you are likely to find value.

The size of the spread is noteworthy. It is most pronounced at the earliest stages, when the most teams remain in the cup. This is one of two good reasons for avoiding the early rounds of the FA Cup. The other is what makes it interesting: the sound of falling giants. The famous unpredictability is a graveyard for the gambler. I ran an experiment early on during 2002's FA Cup. Using a spreadsheet, I placed theoretical bets on the half-dozen teams that were dominating the Premiership. They were all expensive, even at the start, but one of them was likely to emerge as the winner and several others, I thought, would make it to the final rounds. Leeds and Man U were knocked out early. Liverpool were matched with Arsenal and went out. I abandoned the project as the losses spiralled. There is little value to be had. Arsenal, the eventual winners, were 28 to buy even before the third round, when there were sixty-four teams left in the competition and there was no way of knowing who they would meet in the fourth round. Arsenal made up at 80 for winning the competition, a poor return for the risks. Leeds were also priced at 28 and made up at 0. Liverpool were 29 and Man U 27; both made up at 5 for thumping losses.

Better value might lie in special markets bookmakers sometimes run on the number of Premiership teams booted out in the early stages. This is true in any competition that depends either on a knock-out stage or a few matches. It is tempting to pick winners early on, but treacherous. Roma were tipped as strong contenders for the Champions League and were priced to make it past the quarter-finals. They never made it out of the second group stage. When the competition resumed after the winter break Juventus had had by far the strongest record in their home competition, winning eight and drawing three in Serie A since November. They also made an early exit. An even more extreme case came some months later in the World Cup. Before it started people were buying favourites France and Argentina at 48 points in the tournament's 100 Index, which meant the teams had to make the semi-finals, worth 50 points, before you broke even. Both made up at zero, failing to make it out of the group.

Even those teams that did well, such as Brazil, were better value in other markets such as Total Tournament Goals, individual players' tournament Goal Minutes, or in the 25 Index for their group.

Multiple markets mean multiple ways to play the same result. Look for the best value. When England played Denmark, bookmakers offered Time of First Goal to buy at 41 minutes – and 'Time the score will be 0–0' to sell at 43. An easy arbitrage.

The phenomenon is certainly not confined to football.

England were made overwhelming favourites in the Six Nations, priced at 55 in a 60 index before the first face had been pressed into the mud. A single bad afternoon, losing at the Stade de France, left them second. A spread firm told me later that the smart money, betting from the clients they watch very carefully, had been on France from the start. At just 38 to buy they certainly offered much better value. What is the point of buying a team at 55 in a 60 index before the tournament starts? That's a final-round price.

Nevertheless, the FA Cup is an extreme example. It is easy to see why, especially in the modern game. The biggest teams are struggling to manage schedules packed with three competitions. They have already largely given up on the fourth, the Worthington Cup. The Champions League and the Premiership are considered the most important, not least because there is less danger of an early, humiliating exit. So in the early rounds, no matter what they say, the top clubs are not going to be as focused as the smaller clubs. Only in the later rounds, when the prize is within sight, does that change.

It is the night before the quarter-finals begin. These feature eight teams, at least in theory. I think they feature only four. Arsenal are playing Newcastle. Chelsea are playing Spurs. The winner will almost certainly come from those four. Arsenal and Newcastle are both flying high and the winner of their match is the likeliest victor of the tournament. Chelsea have a good chance, Spurs a reasonable one.

Fulham are playing West Bromwich Albion, and Middlesbrough face Everton. These are much weaker teams. Although anything can happen in the FA Cup, I want to bet against all four of them.

Most bookmakers offer a 100 index on the FA Cup.

You can sell the four weak teams. West Brom are 42, Fulham 53, Boro 46 and Everton 44. Add those together and you are selling the lot for 185. You are betting the four, between them, will collect fewer points than that. How likely is it that?

The index offers 33 points for a team that is knocked out at this stage, 50 for those knocked out in the semi-finals, 70 for the losing finalist and 100 for the team that wins the trophy. Two of these teams will be knocked out this weekend. They collect 66 points and that is it. This leaves the other two scrabbling to get 119 points between them. If they face Newcastle/Arsenal and Chelsea/Spurs in the next round, they will probably both be knocked out for a total of 100 points, leaving 19 points profit. If they face one another, one will go out (50 points) and one will go through to the final to likely defeat (70 points). That would make up at 120, an insignificant 1-point loss. There are only two risks. The first is that they do not face each other next round. Instead, they face Arsenal or Newcastle and Chelsea or Spurs – and both win. That would ensure them 170 points, and the four teams 236 overall, realising a horrendous 117-point loss. But it is highly unlikely. The second risk is that only one triumphs in the semi-finals but goes on to win the cup. That would produce 216, or a 97-point loss.

There are ways to hedge simply by buying these teams back on the cheap in the fixed odds market. If Fulham beat West Brom and then face Arsenal, the bookies will offer very long odds on the Craven Cottage boys and your risks can be covered.

Middlesbrough and Fulham go through after beating Everton 3–0 and West Brom 1–0. More importantly, the winners are not drawn against one another in the semi-finals. There is an excellent chance to knock out both of them. In the strong half of the draw Chelsea beat Spurs 1–0 and Arsenal defeat Newcastle 2–0 in a rematch. I collect profits from selling Everton and West Brom and double my short position on Boro and Fulham.

For the semi-finals Chelsea are drawn against Fulham in a west London derby thought to be so incendiary that the match is moved to Villa Park. There the two teams with the prominent, naff logos square off. Turning on the TV to watch, I reflect that a Martian landing on Earth would think the match was between Pizza Hut and Emirates. And for once, remarkably, there are no sudden, implausible amendments to the script. The Blues, or Emirates, win 1–0 with a first-half goal from John Terry and Fulham slink off for their pizzas. Arsenal beat Boro 1–0. By the time dawn breaks for the final I have already made my money.

10

A Beautiful Game

This is it. The sun is shining bright, even in Cardiff, as
Arsenal and Chelsea race on to the pitch for what should
be a cracker of an FA Cup Final. The players line up,
hands behind their backs, and the band strikes up what
the announcer calls 'the National Anthem'. What a perfect
showpiece for the English game – except that the match
takes place in Wales and most of the players are from
overseas. They should play 'La Marseillaise', but instead
it's 'God Save the Queen'.

The FA Cup is the busiest day of the year for the bookmakers. It comes during a busy weekend for sports. Betting
is brisk on the World Snooker Championships, a
horseracing festival, a golf tournament and the Scottish
FA Cup Final. The bookmakers are pulling out all the
stops. Sporting Index have fifty staff in the office fielding
bets that afternoon. They are offering 183 markets on the
game.

These range from the standard bets, such as Total Goals,
Supremacy and Multi-corners, all the way to something
called 'Booze Brothers', a special bet on events involving
Arsenal's dried-out captain Tony Adams and Chelsea's

John Terry, an occasional late-night fixture down the Fulham Road. There is a market on Number of Throw-ins (priced at 42 to 45), Goal Kicks (19.5 to 21), Shirt Numbers of Corner Takers, Penalty Goal Minutes, and 'Card Minutes' for a number of players, which adds up the times when players are booked. The bookies have offered a market on which ten-minute spell, from the first ten to the last ten of regular time, will feature the most action. They will rate them according to bookings, goals, corners and so on. There are markets on the goalkeepers. And with a nod to the multinational nature of the sides, there are times offered for First French Goal (for such players as Thierry Henry and Emmanuel Petit), Dutch Goal (Jimmy Floyd Hasselbaink and Dennis Bergkamp), English Goal, Italian Goal and 'Rest of the World Goal'.

You can grow dizzy just counting them. You have to be disciplined working through them, or you will find yourself flipping back and forth helplessly, before placing the wrong bets. Print them out: Sporting's take up eight pages. There are doubtless arbitrage opportunities lurking in there, but finding them will be a challenge. It will not be worth the candle.

Discipline is likely to be a big issue in the game. Some would suggest that making Mike Riley referee for the match is like putting a chain-smoker in charge of an ammu-nition dump. He has the second highest bookings count in the Premiership. On the other hand, red cards are very scarce in FA Cup Finals, and the price for bookings, at 50 to sell, 54 to buy, looks high enough.

I am tempted by Card Minutes for Arsenal's Ray Parlour. His red card against Bayer Leverkusen, reducing the Gunners to ten men in a crucial Champions League match, made it more likely that the Germans would equalise and cost Arsenal a place in the final rounds.

At 24 to buy, Parlour's Card Minutes looks attractive. I reckon a yellow card is a certainty. However, I've seen him get that out of the way early, possibly to give him plenty of time to work on his red. I decide to pass and look elsewhere.

Two intriguing markets are 'Fat Lady' and, an innovation for this match, 'First Lady'. The first (from the old cliché 'It ain't over till the fat lady sings') gives points for events in the last ten minutes of regular time. Goals and red cards are worth 15 points each, yellow cards 5 points and corners 3. Points are doubled for anything occurring in the 88th minute. Fat Lady is priced at 14 to sell, 17 to buy. More attractive is First Lady, which does exactly the same for the first ten minutes. Sporting also offers double points for events in the 1st minute, a pointless exercise as you will be lucky if you get a throw-in that quickly. First Lady is priced at 8 to 11. I believe the game is likely to start slowly as the two teams test each other out cautiously. Everyone is nervous at the start of a big match like this, no matter how experienced. I sell First Lady at 8. It would take a corner (3 points) and a yellow (5 points) in the first ten minutes to erase my profits. I am prepared to take the chance.

Although the market Time of First Throw-in has disappeared, Stop at a Corner is almost as good. You get a point for every throw-in before the first corner. Initially this was priced at 5.5 to 7, but punters have been piling in and shortly before kick-off it is 7 to 9. I decide to go against the weight of money and sell. In the time it takes me to place the bet online, the sell price moves to 7.5 so I get a better deal. I have no specific data, but seven throw-ins before a corner sounds like a lot. I keep the bet small.

My third stop is my favourite player, Freddie

Ljungberg. In the absence of Robert Pires, Ljungberg has become the star of the Arsenal line-up. He is scoring effectively a goal a game at the moment, and threatens persistently. I ignore Player Performance, which is hard to measure by the eye, and look at Goal Minutes. There he is priced at 16 to buy, ludicrously cheap. Thierry Henry's Goal Minutes are priced far higher, at 27 to buy, but he has not been on form in recent weeks. As always, the big-name strikers look overpriced because they attract a lot of amateur money. Chelsea's Jimmy Floyd Hasselbaink is 21 to buy, even though he is injured and might not make the match. That shows you the silliness of some prices. On a day when Arsenal are deemed to have the advantage anyway, is an injured Hasselbaink more likely to score than a fit Ljungberg? Freddie's Goal Minutes are more attractive than his price in the 25-point First-Last Blast, where he is 6 to buy. He tends to warm up as the game goes along and to score late. Others clearly have the same idea. Ljungberg's price has risen to 17 minutes by the time I buy. After placing my bet I have second thoughts and double it.

There remain the joke markets, such as 'Booze Brothers' and 'Chelsea Village People'. Two days earlier I had lunch with two pals, Jocky and Joseph (which, come to think of it, sounds like a Channel 4 comedy duo). Joseph, a high-powered analyst who spends his days predicting where the next Enron will come from, argues these are all sells. 'There are no natural "shorts",' he said. 'Pretty much everyone who bets on these markets is a buyer, so they must be overpriced.' Certainly, the book-makers are aware that they are likely to end up carrying the short position themselves, so they are likely to price them high. On the phone the day before the match with Wally Pyrah, a good-natured director at Sporting, I put this to him. He chortled, then said, 'I suspect you're right.'

Chelsea Village People is simply an artificial market on the Chelsea performance. You get 1 point for every completed Chelsea pass in the Arsenal half, a point for every minute Chelsea leads, 10 points every time the Chelsea trainer comes on the pitch, 10 points every time Chelsea are booked for shirt pulling, 25 every time Chelsea go into the lead if they end up losing the match, and 25 points if Emmanuel Petit is seen on TV touching his long, flowing blond hair. To buttress the Village People tag, Sporting have given camp titles, such as 'Queen of the South', for individual prices.

If you want to analyse a new or unfamiliar market, break it down into its components. There are three material factors here: completed passes, leading minutes and the trainer's appearance. In a worst-case scenario Chelsea could lead for eighty minutes, complete a hundred passes and the trainer might come on three times. That would make up at 210, but would be extraordinary. We should ignore shirt pulling. If Chelsea surrender a lead it would be surprising, and if that happened, costing 25 points, it would inevitably knock time off their leading minutes anyway. And forget Petit's hair. Do you really think Sporting Index has sat down and watched lots of Chelsea footage to see how often the French midfielder plays with his locks? It's thrown in to distract you, and to tempt people who fancy some fun. The price for Chelsea Village People is 175, which is close enough to my worst-case scenario to make it a sell.

And finally comes the 'Scrabble' market, which adds up the Scrabble points of every goal scorer's name. Zola is 13 points – Z, as anyone who has played the board game knows, is 10 points and the other three letters are 1 apiece. The bookie does not give double- or triple-word scores, alas. This is an intriguing market. How many points is Hasselbaink worth? K is 4 points, I think, as is B – or is it 3? And what about Bergkamp? And Ljungberg? Where's my Scrabble set? I'm hunting for the board half an hour before kick-off when I remember it is in the hallway cupboard. The locked hallway cupboard. Where's the key? I am hunting for the key when I reach a decision.

To hell with it. When in doubt sell the gimmick market. Am I going to spend my life hunting for Scrabble boards just before the FA Cup Final? A price of 39 seems to imply at least three goals anyway. I sell.

Then I settle in at the local to watch the game. Within two minutes of kick-off a clumsy tackle by Ray Parlour earning him a yellow card is a double-edged sword: it justifies my decision to avoid his Card Minutes but also loses me 5 points on First Lady, where I had bet on an uneventful first ten minutes.

My Stop at a Corner bet quickly proves more dangerous than I thought. I am hoping for a corner before there have been seven throw-ins, but from the whistle the ball is being hoofed, scrambled and deflected out of bounds before it nears either end. After what seems an age, but is actually less than ten minutes, the ball goes out for a corner. I assumed that there were ten throw-ins – I lost count – but it made up at only seven for a tiny profit.

The game drags on. Mike Riley, after some early action, slows down with the cards (the Bookings market eventually makes up at 50, bang on the opening sell price). Arsenal and Chelsea both have good attacks halted for offsides that turn out, on replay, to have been mistaken. The north Londoners play below their best. Bergkamp, after an early missed header, seems to vanish. By early in the second half Chelsea are getting the better of the game, attacking with vigour and defending tightly, while Arsenal are looking distinctly ropy at the back. Parlour is passing with unerring accuracy to opponents. Gooner hearts are in their mouths when a spectacular strike by Gudjohnsen from outside the area is only just turned over the bar by David Seaman.

Arsenal are penned in their own half. Whenever they regain possession, they quickly give it back. Their counter-attacks start in promising style but peter out. In the 70th minute they are doing it again. Ray Parlour is caught up just outside the Chelsea box: he made a good run through midfield, but he's held it too long and he's missed his chance. Defenders converge. He steps free, turns and shoots – and the ball sweetly curls into the top right-hand corner of the box. One–nil to the Arsenal.

Ray Parlour. Ray Parlour! Good Lord. In the bar my fellow Gooner James is jumping up and down – and shouting at me, accusingly, 'And you said Parlour was useless!'

The only possible explanation, I reason, is that Parlour was trying to kick the ball out for a Chelsea goal-kick but hooked the shot. After the match he seemed as astonished as everybody else that he had scored.

Ray Parlour. You could have bought his Goal Minutes at 6.

The goal came against the run of play, and Chelsea fight back with spirit. Within moments they appear to equalise, but the goal is disallowed for reasons that are drowned out by uproar in the bar. This seems to knock the wind out of them. And then, in the 78th minute, breaking from midfield . . .

Excuse me. Could we have a drum roll, please?

. . . Freddie Ljungberg weaves past and around the defenders and finishes with style, bending the ball around

Cudicini to make it 2–0 to the Arsenal.

And to conjure up some juicy profits for me.

The perfect game. Chelsea Village People made up at 168. This shows how far out I was – Chelsea did not lead for a single minute, yet it made up just 7 below the sell price. I was lucky to make it out without a hefty loss, never mind with a profit. Silly markets might be over-priced, or they might not. There is really no way to tell. In future I will leave them alone unless I have enough facts to make an informed decision.

First Lady made up at 8, a half-point loss. Stop at a Corner made up at 7 for a minute, half-point profit. And Scrabble? It made up at 29, a juicy 11-point profit, thanks to Ray Parlour, my new best buddy. In among the Zolas, Gudjohnsens, Hasselbainks and Bergkamps, Parlour proved a good, dull, Anglo-Saxon name, worth all of 9 points in Scrabble. Thank heavens for the English.

11

Final Whistle

Four days later, Arsenal completed the double by winning at Old Trafford. In a packed London bar, half the punters fell silent and the other half went wild. James, the Gooners' Gooner, sank to his knees and began sobbing.

Football is a tough market to beat. Prices are set by level-headed market-makers, and they know their stuff. Some of their prices turn out to be spectacularly wrong, but over time they are making money. It is possible to follow suit. There are a number of principles that will fatten your profits and trim your losses if you follow them.

Let the market-makers do the work for you. I'm lazy, I don't want to spend a day running numbers on a game, calculating the probability of corners or bookings. The market-makers have already done this. The results, usually, are reflected in the initial prices. These appear on the bookmakers' websites, though you might need to catch them early. They also feature in the morning's copy of the *Racing Post*. Then compare the prices with those just before the game.

They will have moved, thanks to the weight of money pouring in. You can often make money by simply betting against that movement. Over time this is likely to prove profitable. 'Before kick-off, seventy per cent of punters will be buyers,' says David Garbacz. 'If you wait until just before the game, the prices will be massively inflated. There's a lot of value to be had in opposing these moves.'

'Your clever punters are the ones who oppose the weight of money. They know the price is wrong,' says Patrick Burns, a trader at IG Index.

The weight of money, though, does not always move in predictable ways. The English public, on the whole, struggles to assess overseas teams sensibly. It tends to assume that strong foreign teams, such as Roma, Real Madrid or Germany, are invincible. It also assumes that weaker foreign teams are completely useless. When Liverpool hosted Roma at Anfield last season in a must-win Champions League match the market-makers at the spread firms took a good look at both teams' form and favoured the Reds. The Supremacy price was 0.7 to buy. The public took a deeply gloomy view of Liverpool's chances and sold heavily. The Supremacy price dropped to 0.3 just before kick-off. This was a chance to buy them on the cheap. The bookmakers were right about who had the advantage, although even they underestimated the margin as Liverpool went on to win 2–0. At the start of the 2002 World Cup, the price on England actually fell to counterbalance heavy betting on France and Argentina. Yet after the English beat Argentina, populist opinion swung behind the team. When England played mighty Brazil, they were 11 to buy in the Win Index, nearly level with the South Americans on 14.

When the English rugby team played Wales at Twickenham in the Six Nations they were initially given a thumping Supremacy of 33 points. Wales were a weak team. The English team, despite a surprise loss to France, were exceptionally strong. The punters, who tend to shy away from seemingly high prices, sold heavily. 'They reason the actual make-up can only go so high,' says Patrick Burns. 'People want to limit their risk, so they prefer to sell.' The price plummeted to just 25 by the kick-off. The boys at the desks were smart: England won by 40 points. If you're lazy, you can try just betting against the heaviest price movements in the most popular markets.

Know the numbers and look for value. The team that wins the Premiership is worth, on average, a Supremacy of 1.5 goals at home. That drops to just 0.5 on the road. The Bookings average is 35 in England but 60 in Spain's La Liga. The average goal time is around 50 minutes, so a price for Total Goal Minutes of 150 assumes three goals. If Total Goals is offered at 2.6, that offers better value.

The easiest way to find an edge is to watch the game. Ten minutes' play will tell you more about what is likely to happen in the ninety than ten hours' research and analysis beforehand. Supposed grudge matches turn out to be friendly, with players on both sides laughing and joking with one another. Matches widely written off in advance as a dull encounter provide fireworks from kick-off. The bookmakers, so ready to take a position before-hand, adjust their prices very slowly once the game begins and focus on providing two-way trade. This is why I prefer markets that can be traded in the running, such as Corners (rather than Multi-corners) and Bookings. You can spot a trend first, trade in and then get out for a profit before the half-time whistle.

See what is happening, not what is supposed to happen. This sounds so obvious, but is sometimes very hard to do. Ten minutes into France's do-or-die third game in the World Cup, striker David Trezeguet tried an awkward shot when there was an easy cross available to Sylvain Wiltord, standing in front of an open goal. It was an amateur error. The French players had largely given up. But the prices still showed them favourites to win.

There is sometimes a fine balance between class and form. The United States outplayed Germany in the World Cup, but their strikers hesitated fatally in the penalty box and German keeper Oliver Kahn kept a clean sheet. Belgium pressed Brazil hard, but a typical moment of genius from Rivaldo settled the encounter.

Be cautious about markets that can turn on a single event. The most popular markets are Total Goals and Supremacy, but these leave you vulnerable. Time and again I have bought a team cheaply in the Win Index when it is just one goal down and there are fifteen minutes left on the clock. I have made the trade when the team going cheap is fighting back and creating good chances. The last quarter of an hour, after all, produces the most goals. Sometimes I make money; more often I lose it. It's a pure gamble.

Make only one bet per game. This is an excellent discipline. It will prevent you from frittering away cash on losing bets. We always painfully remember the big losses, but the trickle effect of smaller ones arguably does more damage. Your marginal calls will be weaker than the one you like the most, so stick to the one you like the most.

Only bet on games you are watching. You are trying to pit your wits against the market. If you aren't watching, you might just as well flip a coin. And if you can't commit ninety minutes to a game, why should you commit money?

Be selective. The bookies have one big advantage over you: the spread. But you have one advantage over them: you don't have to bet on every market for every game. 'We have the disadvantage of having to make up all these different markets,' admits a dealer. 'The research that goes into the last of them is just too flimsy. Mistakes are made. We can't watch them all closely, especially on big games.'

The wisest bets you will place will be the ones you skip. Don't give up this advantage easily. Herbert Yardley, author of the card-game classic *The Education of a Poker Player*, said if a player knows what he is doing he chucks in six hands out of seven. He only plays when he is convinced he will win – and even then he won't win them all. Warren Buffett, who has made £20 billion from the stock market, often says there are no 'called strikes' in investing. (A called strike is a baseball term referring to when a batter gets called out for not swinging at the ball.) The same is true for speculating – and gambling.

Specialise. If you focus on a few markets, you will give yourself an edge over all the generalists. 'The most successful punters concentrate on a couple of markets, like Shirt Numbers, Corners or Bookings,' says Patrick Burns at IG. 'I tend to bet on Shirt Numbers and Bookings. I like Shirt Numbers because there's a lot of information. These are the markets where the prices can be wrong. In Total Goals and Supremacies you can also be wrong, but the spread is too wide. These markets offer little value.' A senior market-maker at Sporting Index adds: 'Specialise. Stick to what you know, and what you think you're good at. It's all about being better than us. I'm not saying we're unbeatable. We are.' I know of one gambler who made more than £1,000 betting on athletics, reasoning the bookmakers' expertise was relatively weak. Form in athletics is also consistent. In what other sport can someone win 100 or more competitions in a row?

Before placing a bet, ask yourself, why is the price wrong? Or, to put it another way, what makes you think you are so smart? You might have thought of something the market hasn't. You might know something it doesn't, because you have been following a team closely or have done some investigating of a little-known European team. 'You need to do a little bit of homework,' says David Garbacz. 'Don't just bet blindly. Try to get as much information as possible. Don't bet at nine-thirty in the morning when you can bet at just before kick-off, when you know the names of the players, you know whether Henry's playing or whatever.' Or you might be selling England or Manchester United knowing the fans have been buying with their hearts. A dealer at Sporting admits: 'Total Goals for a Man U game might only be worth 3, but you will put them up to 3.2 because you know people will buy them at that price.' In the Premiership Points market Chelsea have traditionally proved overpriced. The bookmakers attribute that to the Blues' strong following in the Southeast, especially among the City types who make up a sizeable chunk of their clientele. These are all good examples of working out why a price is incorrect, but if you can't think of a reason why the price is wrong, it's probably right.

Always look at your downside before you place a bet. Remember many spread bets offer potentially unlimited risk. So if it all goes wrong, how much will you lose? If the answer is too much, you can take steps to minimise your risk. The steps are straightforward. Be wary of going short. When you do, prefer capped Index markets to open-ended ones such as Supremacy or Total Goals. If you must sell in an open-ended market, keep your stakes small, watch the game, and move swiftly to cut your losses. Take the pain and live to fight another day. Don't sell an open-ended market which is not offered in running.

Most bookmakers also offer some stop-loss facilities which limit your risks. These cap potential profits and potential losses from individual bets. As the industry is still changing rapidly, it is worth asking when you apply for forms. Some facilities only apply on certain accounts. Check the details. At IG, a stop-loss limits not the make-up, but the multiple of your stake that you can lose. Under this scheme, if you sell a cricket team's total runs at 100 with a stop-loss at 250, you will not be stopped out until the runs hit 350 – or 250 higher than where you sold.

Amateurs always run their losses and cut their profits. Professionals do the reverse. Jonathan Sparke says, 'Look at your potential losses before you count your profits. Look at selling before you look at buying – most people are buy-prone. Do your research. Only bet on subjects you know about. If you're going to bet on a rugby international, get the weather forecast. Always know what the average expectation is and then look at what conditions apply which might move the result higher or lower. Trade where you have an edge, some specialised knowledge. Don't "average" into adversity. When events run against you, don't double your bet at the seemingly cheaper price. Clients are always doing this, and increasing their even-tual losses. Afterwards you get the bleating call, saying "I can't believe how unlucky I was." The typical client also cuts his profits too quickly. Instead run your profits, and cut your losses.'

On the whole, averaging is foolhardy. It usually means you are betting with your heart rather than your head. That is the fastest route to perdition, if you are lost. It's also a con. If you sold Total Goals at 3, selling more at 4 does not change your initial bet. A losing bet is a losing bet. You might have made a mistake, or you might have been unlucky, or circumstances might have changed. When Mark Ramprakash walked to the crease in the Oval Test of the 2001 Ashes series the Australian bowlers led by Shane Warne were slicing through the English order. The light was dim and the cloud cover gave the swingers plenty of movement. Ramprakash looked nervous and uncertain. When he was on 5 I sold his total runs at 39. That was around his average for the series so far and he did not look like this was going to shape up for a better-than-average performance. Indeed, he was nearly out several times soon after the bet. But the clouds slowly dispersed, the light improved, the bowlers slowed and his confidence grew. With painful slowness he eventually reached his half-century, by which time I had to admit the circumstances had changed: I had made the right bet, but ended up with the wrong result. That is not a contradiction. So I bought his runs back, well into the high 80s, and doubled my stake as I went long of his runs. He ended the day going strong at 124 not out, only to fall early the following morning to Glenn McGrath for 133. I made back nearly all my losses. Don't get married to a point of view. When the circumstances change, so should your opinion. Always chase the best price. These can vary considerably across bookmakers. Getting the best value will make a huge difference over time.

Look hardest for value in the long-term markets. The bookmakers take most of their money on individual games, and these absorb most of their attention. Think about your own job. What gets more attention – things that might be important, or things which are urgent? These guys will lose a fortune if they screw up a price on Wednesday's big game. The UEFA Cup 100 Index, and even the Premiership Golden Boot Index, is way down their list of priorities. David Garbacz says, 'Where companies tend to lose money is in the long-term markets, like Premiership Points and the Golden Boot. There's too much to keep an eye on. The long-term markets are where punters have an edge. The market-makers tend to get a little bit bored. I hated them.'

Long-term markets have an additional advantage – they are less prone to individual freak events. You can spot trends. More importantly, if you look in the right place, you can spot them before anyone else does and make good money.

Never bet with your heart. Betting with your head is good. Betting with your gut (instinct) is acceptable, and it sometimes makes better calls than your head. But betting with your emotions is to take the express elevator to gamblers' hell. If you are hoping, wishing and praying for a result, don't bet on it too. Just enjoy the game. This is one of the reasons I prefer the Bookings and Corners markets to Supremacies. It is impossible to get emotional about corners, no matter how hard you try. Once you bet on who will win, you will start cheering for them. This will leave you in a poor state to recognise when the game's up.

It sounds absurdly obvious, but make sure you know what you are betting on. Even the simplest markets vary across different sports. For example the Win Index in tennis reflects the score as well as who won, and can make up between 25 and -25.

Look first for value in selling. Punters, on the whole, prefer to buy, it is much more enjoyable, so prices tend to be skewed to the upside on such markets as Bookings, Shirt Numbers and Total Goals. The arrival of more sophisticated gamblers is eroding this bias, but it still exists. David Garbacz says, 'In all my years, as a general rule, the seller does better than the buyer. It's getting slightly less like that, but eighty per cent of my trades are still sells.'

Be wary of markets with big spreads, like Supremacy and Total Goals. It is that much harder to make money. Unless there is a specific, compelling reason to choose one of these markets, you are usually better off in the Win Index, Shirt Numbers and Goal Minutes.

Be aware of the most common gambler's mistakes. We all tend, instinctively, to overvalue long shots and accumulators. We also misjudge the role of pure luck. We assume when we win that we were clever. We assume when we lose that we were unlucky. This is often true, but not always.

Finally, don't let the blizzard of prices and markets distract you from the obvious. When Bill Clinton ran for US President in 1992 the country was in deep recession so he had a sign stuck prominently on his campaign headquarters that read: 'It's the economy, stupid.' It reminded him of what to focus on whenever other issues threatened to distract him. When betting, it's easy to get lost in the prices and forget the obvious. When this happens, you tend to shy clear of apparently high prices even though they are justified. You end up buying the Goal Minutes of a no-hope defender at 10, even though a striker like Jimmy Floyd Hasselbaink is likely to prove better value at 20. One trader admits, 'We have one clever punter who almost always buys. He will pay high prices for things, but he's a very good judge of football.'

Think about the game and look at the form guide before you look at prices. Only place a bet if it looks cheap and if you were interested in it *before* looking at prices. Remember, it's the football, stupid.

Appendices

I

Research

Anyone looking for an extra edge will need to do some homework before the game. The football punter today faces an embarrassment of riches in his search for information. For the Premiership, a good handbook before the season starts is the *Opta Yearbook*. This gives detailed studies of each team's performance in the previous season and some thoughts on the likely effect of changes in the off season.

If you are looking to bet on a game, grab the *Racing Post* in the morning. It usually contains several pages on football. In addition to the analysis, which you can take or leave, it contains all sorts of juicy data, including the number of goals each team scores and lets in per game, average bookings figures and players' shirt numbers. This is especially useful for European matches, when the opposing team's figures might be unknown to you. It also contains the antepost prices from the four big spread firms. I find it useful to keep the relevant page of the *Post* with me when watching a game. You can tell at a glance the possible impact on Shirt Numbers of every substitution, it reminds you who the danger men are for each team, and tells you where the prices for each market started out. This can give you a pretty good idea of how far events on the field are being reflected.

You might also subscribe to *Sports Adviser*, a weekly magazine specialising in sports betting. It has a lot of coverage of spread betting. It also has a website (www.sportsadviser.com), which offers tips for the day and even a penny share-style 'chat forum' where people trade opinions and ideas. The website needs a subscription; they will bundle that and the magazine together. Another website, www.onewaybet.com, specialises in spread betting. Edited by financial journalist Angus McCrone, it mainly covers the financial markets but is moving into the sports arena. I have to declare an interest here, as during the World Cup I wrote a spread betting column for onewaybet.com.

The internet, of course, is the best resource available. Go to Soccerbase (www.soccerbase.com), which will give you almost everything you need to know, certainly for English and Scottish games. For upcoming matches it offers a 'Spread betting stats' link which lays out average goals overall, home and away for each team, average time of first goal, bookings, recent record and the form of the leading goal-scorers. Go to the home page and click on the 'vs' between the names of the two teams playing. It also usually gives data on the average corner numbers, although for some odd reason it occasionally omits this, and details on the referee, including his average bookings make-up.

If you click on the referee's name it will show you his bookings make-up by match for the past season, with the option of looking at earlier seasons too if you so desire. His recent record can be important: a high average bookings count can be skewed by one wild match, or by some heavy card-waving early in the season, or in lower leagues where games can be more volatile. This can offer a golden, and profitable, opportunity to sell Bookings, where the price is likely to reflect his overall average.

Soccerbase offers a wealth of other information, including season points tables for all the British leagues, and records for this season and past for teams and individual players. This is, incidentally, one of the key sites used by the spread firms. It also, unusually, runs on a quick server. There are many websites around that have benefited from a lot of thought, offering loads of useful data and good layouts, which are then rendered virtually unusable because they are apparently powered by hamsters on treadmills. *Fat* hamsters. Even the bookmakers' web pages, which on the whole are well laid-out, are agonisingly slow. If you want to place bets online during a game, you really have to log on to the site before kick-off and keep the internet connection open throughout the match. Even then it is a rush to place your bet before the prices move.

Sporting Life runs an excellent website (www.sporting life.com), which is all that remains of the venerable newspaper. This is one of the fastest ways of getting the latest news, including live half-time scores. It gives match reports, including a reasonable archive, fixtures lists and detailed team analyses. It also contains some outstanding analysis that is hard to find elsewhere. Click, for example, on 'Premiership' down the left-hand side and then click on 'Stats'. Here you can find out team performances over the season broken down by first- and second-half records, disciplinary records and ratings for each team's attack and defence – although when I checked those pages the two columns, showing goals scored or conceded home and away, were the wrong way round. Sporting Life's website also includes useful match previews and, for those who can't get near a TV, live in-the-running updates from big matches. The *Racing Post* (www.racingpost.co.uk, or www.smartbet.co.uk) also has a very good website that includes the latest news, predictions, tips and analysis.

There is a desperate paucity of websites that will guide you before a Champions League game. Form in domestic leagues does not always correspond to form in the big one, for obvious reasons. Teams playing domestically are overall up against weaker opponents. In Europe they all tend to try to raise their games. Home-field advantage matters more, and differently. And many teams will give different priorities to different competitions, for example resting injured players in league matches in the hope that they will be fit for European games.

The first port of call before any European game is Uefa's excellent site, www.uefa.com. It includes useful analysis and team reports, records, standings and fixtures lists. Click on the name of the relevant competition, listed down the left-hand side, and follow the links from there. Alas, nowhere could I find a simple explanation of how the draw works in the Uefa Cup and the Champions League or how teams with seemingly equal records are separated.

Second stop should be the website maintained by statistics specialists Opta (www.opta.co.uk). This has information on the English and Scottish Premierships, Italian Serie A, German Bundesliga, Spain's La Liga, the Dutch League and the Champions League. For the nitty-gritty on European leagues it is unmatchable, offering team rankings by goal scoring, tackling, passing, shooting, crossing, discipline, and individual player rankings by most of the same criteria. The data on the Champions League, where for example teams tend to pick up fewer cards than in domestic league games, is vital. There is also invaluable information on national referees.

The site shows not only the number of red and yellow cards per game, whether by team or by referee, but the number of fouls per card. This is especially useful for working out how dirty a team is or how strict a referee is. Foul numbers are more consistent than bookings. If one referee gives a free-kick for a particular tackle, the chances are good that most other referees would respond the same way. That is not true for cards. So if a referee takes fewer fouls to show a card, this is strong evidence he is playing tough.

For European league games, visit Alpha Soccer. The home page can be found at www.alphasoccer.com. Click on 'League Tables' at the top and you are taken to a new page. Down the left-hand side is listed virtually every league around the world, from Australia to Yugoslavia. Follow the links and you can find league tables, home and away data, full results details and information on forthcoming fixtures. Position your cursor over the name of any team, without clicking, to get the latest form.

Soccerbot (www.soccerbot.com) is useful, especially for European matches. It includes details about every national competition, including current tables, live prices, top scorers, recent form and even some predictions.

SoccerStats (www.soccerstats.com) gives similar data to Soccerbase. It covers more national leagues but in less detail. Interestingly, it offers an (apparently) sophisticated predictions service for each match. These appear to be based on Poisson distributions, a complex mathematical technique relating to probability. Click on 'Statistics' on the left-hand side. On the next page click on 'Stats and

Picks', which should be highlighted next to the particular league that interests you. On the page that follows that scroll down to the bottom. Click on 'Details' next to the match that interests you for more statistics.

Peerless for its in-the-running coverage of a match, for those unable to get to a TV, is www.sports.com. Alone of the website operators they have worked out that most people do not have a fast LAN connection at home. On one page their live coverage gives two-minute updates, the list of players on the pitch and current data on the number of goals, attempts, corners, cards and even offsides. Sports.com went into administration as this book was being prepared, and a question mark, alas, hangs over its future. This is inevitable with the internet. New sites will start up, and others will close down, so this survey can only be of partial use.

During the World Cup I also discovered the outstanding www.talksport.net, which also has a wealth of information for the dedicated punter.

Football365, which floated itself on the stock market during the dotcom boom and where Danny Kelly was a director, runs a chattier site primarily aimed at fans rather than punters. The server sometimes runs very slowly, which makes it frustrating. As for the company, anyone who bought shares should steer clear of gambling, and should probably sign their remaining pounds over to their spouses for safe keeping.

Visit www.soccer-spain.com and www.spanish-soccer.com for a full list of Spanish fixtures, squad details and match reports, including the performance of Spanish teams in international competitions such as the Champions League. Those investigating Germany's lively Bundesliga should visit www.germansoccer.net, which contains detailed results, standings and analysis of forthcoming matches. It also predicts the likely starting line-ups in forthcoming games, useful for those betting on Shirt Numbers, Hot Shots and Players' Goals and Performances. Market-makers also recommend www.marca.com for La Liga, www.kicker.de for the Bundesliga, and www.italian-soccer.com for Serie A.

If you are serious about punting, you should sign up for some of the free email newsletters available. These can save an enormous amount of time and ensure you get the analysis and stats you need before the game. Sign up for SpreadMail (www.spreadmail.com) run by Sporting Index. This gives you the antepost prices. Also put your name down for the excellent AlphaSoccer email. On the home page (www.alphasoccer.com) click on 'Betting Guide' at the top. On the new page click on 'Betting Newsletter' near the bottom on the left. This is a wonderful service, completely free at the time of writing. Each email previews forthcoming matches, talks about recent form, injuries and changes to the squad, and gives you the best available prices on each outcome in the fixed odds market. If you are looking for arbitrage against a spread, or simply want a flutter, this can be useful. Soccerstats (www.soccer stats.com) also offers a useful email. At the home page click on 'Mailing List' on the left-hand side and follow instructions.

2

Practicalities

The old bookmaking shops have one advantage over spread betting firms. They let you walk in off the street and place a bet. Setting up a spread betting account is an irritating process, made worse by the role of the regulatory Financial Services Authority. You will need to call up to order forms, which you have to return with a cheque and various proofs of identification. These include a utility bill, a bank statement and a photocopy of your passport, to prevent Osama bin Laden from laundering his millions by betting on Real Madrid in the Champions League. The whole process will take a week or ten days.

This is nominally because spread betting can involve unlimited risk, and the firms need sureties to avoid ending up with lots of bad debts. But it is perfectly possible to place limited-risk spread bets. As mentioned already, most offer accounts that build in an automatic stop loss on some or all bets. The real reason is that the Financial Services Authority, a new super-regulator which has taken over half of Docklands, needs to find something to do to justify its massive bureaucracy. Bin Laden can still launder his money, provided he can obtain a fake passport and a gas bill.

If you have a deposit account, you have to give the spread firms a cheque in advance. It operates like a simple bank account. Any losses are automatically debited from the account and any profits are added to it. Some firms will not let you place bets that might exceed your deposit. This can be irritating, especially if you punt on long-term markets such as Premiership Points, where a large amount of your deposit will be notionally held against the purely theoretical maximum loss, in case Manchester United finish the season with zero points or (if you have sold them) Fulham have romped home with the maximum 114.

However, as I said, I am a fan of deposit accounts, at least for occasional gamblers. They provide a useful discipline, prevent you having too many bets open at once, and stop you betting more than you would be willing to lose. If you open an account with £1,000, no matter how carried away you get during a racy Champions League match that is all you can lose.

Once you have opened your account, you will be given a dealing number to call, an account number and a password for online dealing. When you call to place a bet the trader will ask for your account number and your name. The first few times they are likely to ask for your address as well for security purposes, even though someone who has stolen your account number is likely to know your address, too.

You are not required to deal when you call. You can simply ask for prices. At most times the dealers will tell you whatever you want to know. During a game, however, they will generally limit the information to the prices on three markets. This is understandable. I almost never place a bet straight away. I like to think about it for a moment, so I will hang up and then, if I want to deal, call back. Some firms – including, at the time of writing, Sporting Index, but not IG – ask for your name and dealing number before they will even give you prices. This slows you down, and it slows them down. Cynics note that if he takes your account number first, the dealer knows what positions you have before he quotes you a price. This could allow him to anticipate your trade and adjust the price. I have not seen this happen while in dealing rooms, and I suspect you would need to trade in big amounts before the spread firms found this worthwhile. More simply, by taking account numbers first they discourage random call rounds by arbs or those unlikely to trade. But it is counter-productive, wasting a lot of time for clients and dealers. When it happens in the thick of the action during a big game, it is absurd. Always check the price before deciding whether to bet, and after placing the bet repeat to the dealer the bet you have taken: 'Okay, so I've bought Spurs in the Win Index at twelve at ten pounds a point.' The calls are recorded and this will help your case if a mistake is made. I have never, so far at least, had a mistake made over the phone, although one bet placed online apparently disappeared in the ether.

Some markets, such as Total Goals and Supremacy, are quoted in tenths of a goal for the reasons explained earlier. However, place your bets in terms of goals: 'I'll buy Deportivo La Coruña's Supremacy at point seven at one hundred pounds per goal.' Do not say 'per point', because there will then be confusion on both sides about whether you are risking £100 for every goal, or for every tenth of a goal.

The spread firms' websites are where you will find the latest prices. Printing them out makes them easier to look at and compare. The firms also allow dealing online. This has two advantages. The first is that you can see all the prices in front of you. This makes it much easier to make an informed choice. During the game, when prices are moving around a lot, this is attractive. The second is that you can trade in much smaller amounts, because the costs are lower. However, as mentioned earlier, the websites can run slowly.

No matter your wealth or tolerance for risk, start trading initially with the minimum stakes. Some people start by placing theoretical 'mind bets', which allow them to get used to spread betting without risking any cash at all. However, mind bets have the danger that you will ignore your losses and overestimate your gains. Your mind will be more focused on the task in hand, as well as keeping an accurate record of your profits and losses, when you start putting down real money. You can keep things under control by risking as little as £1 a point. The bookies are keen to win new punters, for obvious reasons, and are friendly towards those just starting out. Keep to your minimums for a good period, several months. The tendency is to place a few small bets, win some money, then to start trading in much bigger sums and suffer big losses. You might find that as you become more relaxed about betting you lose concentration and so also start losing money. This is because you will make more marginal bets. Avoiding nine-tenths of the punts that tempt you is a key discipline for speculators. I made nothing but profit for a few weeks, then nothing but losses for several months when I started. If I had escalated my stakes I would be writing this from underneath a bridge. Never bet more than you can afford to lose. And never bet more than you can bear to lose. It's supposed to be fun.

You should open at least two accounts and one of these should be with Sporting Index, which offers the widest choice of bets. Here are the telephone numbers to call, addresses and websites for the main firms:

Sporting Index

www.sportingindex.com

Switchboard: +44 (0)20 7840 4177

Trading (Freephone): 08000 96 96 02

Helpdesk (Freephone): 08000 96 96 07

Helpdesk: +44 (0)20 7840 4050

Address: Sporting Index Ltd, Gateway House, Milverton Street, London SE11 4AP, UK

Email: enquiries@sportingindex.com

IG Index

www.igsport.com

Switchboard: +44 (0)20 7896 0011

Trading (Freephone): 0500 911 911

Helpdesk (Freephone): 0500 913 911

Address: IG Index plc, Friars House, 157–168 Blackfriars Road, London SE1 8EZ, UK

Email: helpdesk@igsport.com

Cantor Index

www.cantorsport.com

Trading (Freephone): 08000 83 7500

Credit Line (Freephone): 08000 83 1116

New Accounts (Freephone): 08000 93 8111

Customer Service (Freephone): 08000 93 8444

Web Support (Freephone): 08000 93 8222

Overseas Trading: + 44 (0)20 7894 7500

Overseas Customer Service: + 44 (0)20 7894 8444

Address: Cantor Sport, 1 American Square, Tower Hill, London EC3N 2LS, UK

Email: cs@cantorsport.co.uk

Spreadex
www.spreadex.com
Freephone: 08000 52 6575
Address: Spreadex Ltd, Freepost ANG 4116, Dunstable,
LU6 1YT, UK

Trading Sports
www.tradingsports.com
Email: info@tradingsports.com
Switchboard: +44 (0)20 8780 6000

Intrade
www.intrade.com
Switchboard: +44 (0)20 7365 9795

The companies' prices can be seen on TV teletext:

Sporting Index: Channel 4, pages 604, 644 (football
only); Channel 4 In-Vision, page 201; Sky Sports, page
361; Sky Digital, pages 681, 682 and 683; Sky In-Vision,
page 381; Reuters and Bloomberg SPIN.

IG Index: Channel 4, page 608; SkyText, page 365; Sky
In-Vision, page 385; ITV In-Vision, page 398; Reuters IGIO.

Cantor Index: Channel 4, page 614; Sky Sports, page
288; Sky Sports In-Vision pages 462 and 463; Reuters
CSPORT; Bloomberg CRIX.

Spreadex: Teletext, page 660; Sky Sports, page 295; Sky
Sports In-Vision, page 299; Reuters SPREADEX.

Tables

Table 1: Win Index/Fixed Odds Conversion

WIN INDEX PRICE (TO BUY)	FIXED ODDS ON WIN	FIXED ODDS ON DRAW
1	24/1	9/1
1.5	47/3	17/3
2	23/2	4/1
2.5	9/1	3/1
3	22/3	7/3
3.5	43/7	13/7
4	21/4	3/2
4.5	41/9	11/9
5	4/1	EVENS
5.5	39/11	9/11
6	19/6	2/3
6.5	37/13	7/13
7	18/7	3/7
7.5	7/3	1/3
8	17/8	1/4
8.5	33/17	3/17
9	16/9	1/9
9.5	31/19	1/19

10	6/4	100[*]
10.5	29/21	95[*]
11	14/11	91[*]
11.5	27/23	87[*]
12	13/12	83[*]
12.5	EVENS	80[*]
13	12/13	77[*]
13.5	23/27	74[*]
14	11/14	71[*]
14.5	21/29	69[*]
15	4/6	67[*]
15.5	19/31	65[*]
16	9/16	63[*]
16.5	17/33	61[*]
17	8/17	59[*]
17.5	3/7	57[*]
18	7/18	56[*]
18.5	13/37	54[*]
19	6/19	53[*]
19.5	11/39	51[*]
20	1/4	50[*]
20.5	9/41	49[*]
21	4/21	48[*]
21.5	7/43	47[*]
22	3/22	45[*]
22.5	1/9	44[*]
23	2/23	43[*]
23.5	3/47	43[*]
24	1/24	42[*]
24.5	1/49	41[*]

[*]Percentage of stake back

Table 2: Average home Supremacy by European league

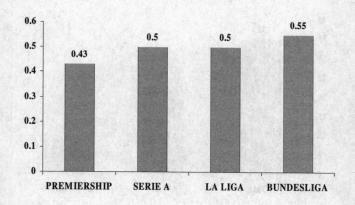

Data: Five seasons, 1997/8–2001/2

Source: www.soccerbase.com

Table 3: Clean sheet percentage

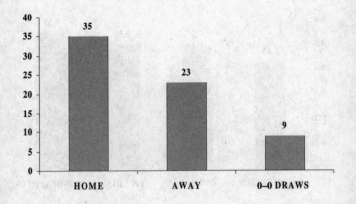

Data: Premiership, ten seasons

Source: Rothmans Football Yearbook 2001–2

Table 4: Home Supremacy by game, Premiership

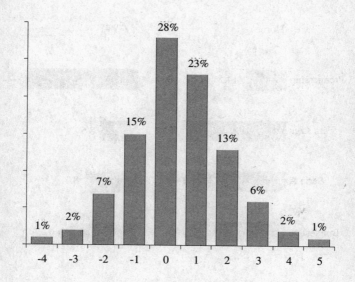

Data: Premiership, ten seasons

Source: Rothmans Football Yearbook 2001–2

Table 5: Average Win Index values by league

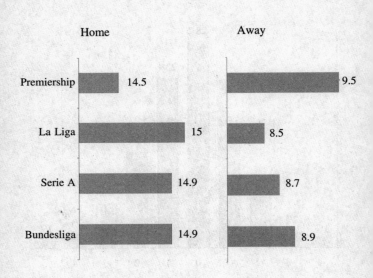

Source: www.soccerbase.com

Table 6: Home win, draw and loss %

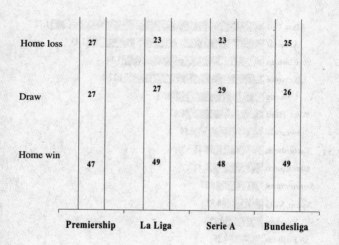

	Premiership	La Liga	Serie A	Bundesliga
Home loss	27	23	23	25
Draw	27	27	29	26
Home win	47	49	48	49

Source: www.soccerbase.com

Table 7: Home-field Supremacy by team, Premiership*

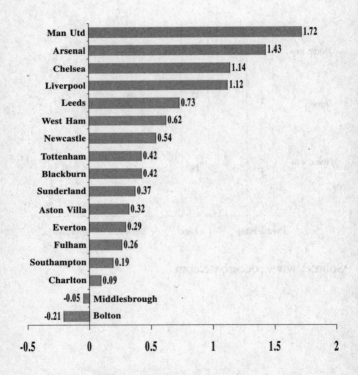

*Average for all Premiership seasons since 1997–8

Source: www.soccerbase.com

Table 8: Home-field Supremacy by team, La Liga*

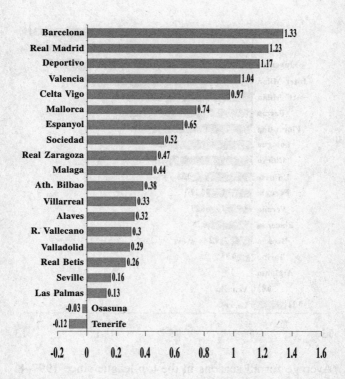

Barcelona	1.33
Real Madrid	1.23
Deportivo	1.17
Valencia	1.04
Celta Vigo	0.97
Mallorca	0.74
Espanyol	0.65
Sociedad	0.52
Real Zaragoza	0.47
Malaga	0.44
Ath. Bilbao	0.38
Villarreal	0.33
Alaves	0.32
R. Vallecano	0.3
Valladolid	0.29
Real Betis	0.26
Seville	0.16
Las Palmas	0.13
Osasuna	-0.03
Tenerife	-0.12

-0.2   0   0.2   0.4   0.6   0.8   1   1.2   1.4   1.6

*Average for all seasons in the top league since 1997–8

Source: www.soccerbase.com

Table 9: Home-field Supremacy by team, Serie A*

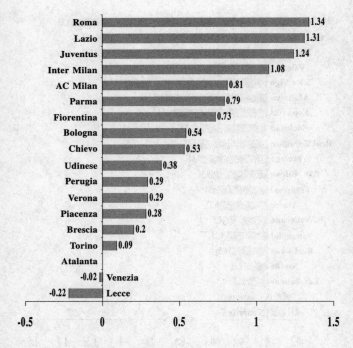

*Average for all seasons in the top league since 1997–8

Source: www.soccerbase.com

Table 10: Home-field Supremacy by team, Bundesliga*

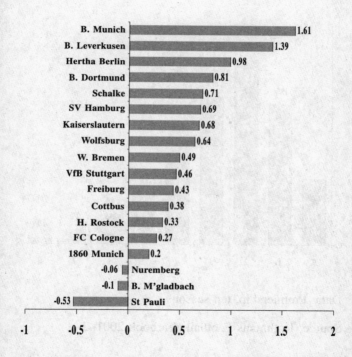

*Average for all seasons in the top league since 1997–8

Source: www.soccerbase.com

Table 11: Total Goals by game

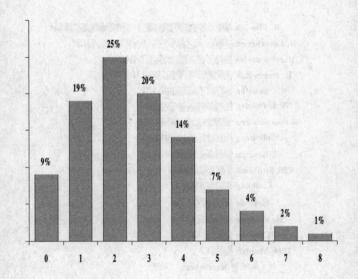

Data: Premiership, ten seasons

Source: Rothmans Football Yearbook 2001–2

Table 12: Goals per 100 games in each five-minute interval

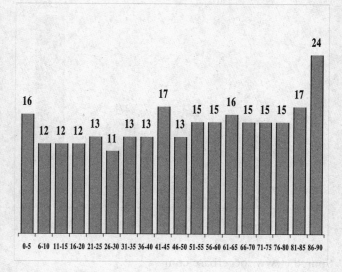

Data: Premiership, four seasons

Table 13: Average Total Goals per game by league

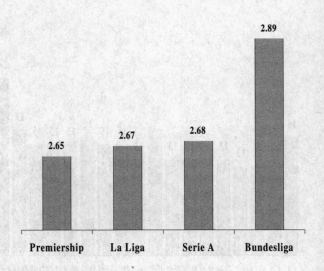

Source: www.soccerbase.com

Table 14: Bookings make-up* per game, Premiership

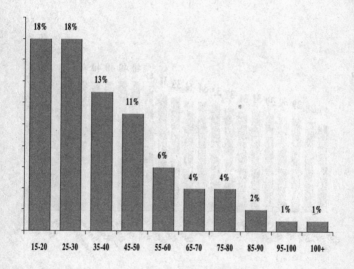

*25 points per red card, 10 points per yellow

Data: Premiership, 2001–2 season
Source: www.soccerbase.com

Table 15: Referee averages per game,* Premiership

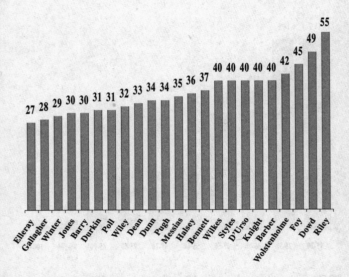

*25 points per red card, 10 points per yellow

Data: Premiership, 2001–2

Source: www.soccerbase.com

Table 16: Average Bookings make-up* per game by league

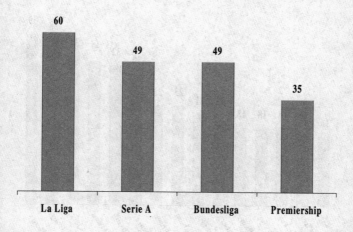

*25 points per red card, 10 points per yellow

Data: Four leagues, 2001–2
Source: www.opta.co.uk

Table 17: Goal Minutes per start,* selected players, 2001–02

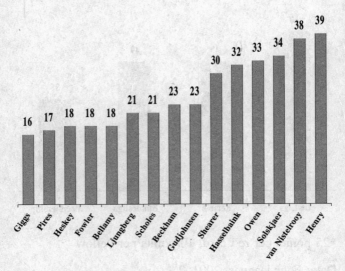

*Premiership only

Data: Premiership, 2001–2 season

Source: www.soccerbase.com

Table 18: Average Goal Minutes per start,* first and second half of the season

(N.B. Players did not necessarily start the same number of games in both halves of the season.)

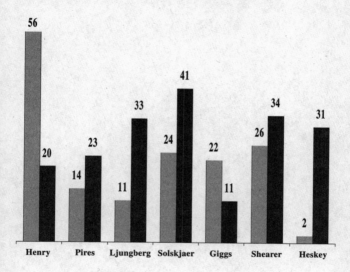

Key: grey = first half
        black = second half

*Premiership only

Data: Premiership, 2001–2 season
Source: www.soccerbase.com